LIVES of the LEFT is a new series of original biographies of leading figures in the European and North American socialist and labour movements. Short, lively and accessible, they will be welcomed by students of history and politics and by anyone interested in the development of the Left. *general editor* David Howell

published: **J. Ramsay MacDonald** Austen Morgan
James Maxton William Knox
Karl Kautsky Dick Geary
'Big Bill' Haywood Melvyn Dubofsky
A. J. Cook Paul Davies
R. H. Tawney Anthony Wright
Thomas Johnston Graham Walker
William Lovett Joel Wiener
Arthur Henderson F. M. Leventhal

forthcoming, to include: **Aneurin Bevan** Dai Smith
Ernest Bevin Peter Weller
Eugene Debs Gail Malmgreen
John MacLean B. J. Ripley and J. McHugh
John Reed Eric Homberger
J. A. Hobson Jules Townshend
George Orwell Stephen Ingle

John Strachey

Michael Newman

Manchester University Press
Manchester and New York

Distributed exclusively in the USA and Canada by St. Martin's Press

Copyright © Michael Newman 1989

Published by Manchester University Press, Oxford Road,
Manchester, M13 9PL, UK
and Room 400, 175 Fifth Avenue, New York, NY 10010, USA

Distributed exclusively in the USA and Canada
by St. Martin's Press, Inc., 175 Fifth Avenue, New York, NY 10010, USA

British Library cataloguing in publication data
Newman, Michael
    John Strachey — (Lives of the left)
    1. Great Britain. Politics. Strachey, John, 1901-1963
    I. Title II. Series
    941.082'3'092'4

Library of Congress cataloging in publication data
Newman, Michael.
    John Strachey / Michael Newman.
        p. cm. — (Lives of the left)
    Bibliography: p.
    Includes index.
    ISBN 0-7190-2174-X. — ISBN 0-7190-2175-8 (pbk.)
    1. Strachey John, 1901-1963. 2. Socialists—Great Britain—Biography.
    I. Title II. Series
    HX244.7.S7N48   1989
    335'.0092'4—dc19
    [B]   89-2494

ISBN 0 7190 2174 X *hardback*
     0 7190 2175 8 *paperback*

Set in Perpetua
by Koinonia Ltd, Manchester

Printed and Bound in Great Britain by
Hartnolls Limited, Bodmin, Cornwall.

For my parents

Contents

	Preface	ix
	Acknowledgements	xi
1	The making of a Socialist (1901–1929)	1
2	In and out of the New Party (1929–1931)	26
3	The thirties: Strachey's golden age	48
4	The break and the reconstruction (1941–1945)	77
5	A government minister (1945–1951)	103
6	*Contemporary Capitalism* (1951–1956)	131
7	The rational anti-Communist (1956–1963)	155
8	Conclusion: Strachey today	179
	Notes	189
	Further reading	199
	Index	203

Preface

In the 1930s John Strachey was pre-eminent as a pro-Communist propagandist and theorist. He was 'probably the most successful and widely-read Marxist who ever wrote in English' —[1] and was almost as well known in the USA as in Britain. He was the driving intellectual force behind the Left Book Club and its most influential writer: his pamphlet, *Why You Should be a Socialist,* sold more than 250,000 copies within two months of its publication in 1938 and was still converting people to the Left in some parts of the world in the early 1960s. By then, however, Strachey himself had long since abandoned Communism and had written a trilogy on democratic socialism, which was also widely regarded as 'the most important contribution to Western socialist thinking of the post-war epoch'.[2]

In addition to his writing, Strachey was active on the Left for forty years. He was involved in a variety of movements, and changed his political perspective several times, before serving as a minister in the 1945–51 Labour governments. When he died in July 1963 he was a member of Labour's front-bench in the House of Commons, and he would certainly have held a cabinet position in Harold Wilson's first administration.

He is thus a particularly fascinating figure, both because it is so rare for British politicians to be theorists and because his intellectual evolution was closely related to the major economic and political changes which took place between 1923 and 1963. In a very real sense, Strachey's shifts in perspective reflect and clarify stages in the development of the British labour movement as a whole.

However, Strachey's reputation has suffered as a result of his volatile political career and because his thought did not fit easily into the normal categories of non-Marxist reformism or Communism. It is, therefore, particularly timely to reassess his contribution. For the acute problems which now confront the labour movement have undermined confidence in both these traditions. Strachey may not have succeeded in resolving the contradictions within socialism, but his sustained attempt to provide a synthesis between reformism and Marxism appears highly relevant today.

This short biography concentrates upon the evolution of his major economic and political ideas in a historical context. It is not sympathetic to all the perspectives which he adopted, but it is written in the firm conviction that he was a highly significant figure who has often been underrated. I am grateful to Manchester University Press for giving me this opportunity to 'set the record straight' on John Strachey.

M.N.

Acknowledgements

I should particularly like to thank the following:

David Howell, for so readily accepting the suggestion of a new study of Strachey and for commenting helpfully on the text; Michael Foot, Lord Douglas Jay and Lord George Strauss for giving me useful interviews in which they offered interpretations of various aspects of Strachey's career and thought; and my friend, Laurence Harris, for discussing economic ideas with me. I would also like to acknowledge the help of the Polytechnic of North London in granting me leave of absence so that I could write the book.

I am extremely grateful to John Strachey's children, Charles and Elizabeth. Not only did they give me access to all their father's material, but they were always happy to talk about him, without ever seeking to influence my judgements.

Above all, I want to thank my whole family. My wife, Ines, gave constant support and encouragement, was always willing to talk about Strachey (yet again) and criticised each draft chapter; and our children, Kate, Hannah and Zack only occasionally complained that I was monopolising the word processor when they wanted to play computer games. I owe a great debt to my parents. My father originally stimulated my interest in the subject by being a Left Book Club activist in the 1930s, and he also commented very constructively on the text; and my mother taught me to argue, question all authority, and type. It is to them that this book is dedicated.

1 The making of a socialist (1901–1929)

John Strachey was an exceptionally complex and contradictory character. He combined extraordinary power and incisiveness as a writer with extreme political volatility; he was both highly theoretical and very emotional; he showed great respect for authority and constantly rebelled against it; he sought complete certainty but never remained sure of his beliefs for long. His strengths and weaknesses both stemmed from these contradictions within his character, and his constant attempt to resolve them in theory or action.

Many of Strachey's inner tensions were the result of his background, for he was an upper-class socialist. He was born into a long-established, privileged family in October 1901. One ancestor had helped Robert Clive to create the British Empire in India, and another, on his mother's side, had been Nassau Senior, the nineteenth-century political economist. His close relatives remained eminent figures in the twentieth-century establishment. His father was St Loe Strachey, the influential owner and editor of the *Spectator*; St Loe's cousins were Lytton Strachey, the historian and critic, and James Strachey, the psychoanalyst and translator of Freud. The list of famous relatives was almost endless and John himself was brought up in an environment which was eminently suitable for a future member of the establishment.

He lived in a comfortable, large house in Surrey under the influence of a nanny, and attended a local preparatory school before going to Eton in 1915 and Oxford (to read History) in 1920. Nor was this all, for St Loe moved in the highest social and political circles, and cabinet ministers, aristocrats and foreign ambassadors were entertained in the Strachey home. John's sister, Amabel, recalled their childhood, without exaggeration, as follows:

> my impression as a child was that if you happened to go to the United States, you would naturally visit the President, or in Egypt the Residency, just as in a fairy-tale you naturally made for the palace of some king or caliph: also that grown-up men – not women of course – were usually MPs and in the cabinet.

She continued, in terms which were very pertinent in relation to Strachey's subsequent development:

> This curious impression was reinforcd year after year... In later life, it affected the way in which both John and I reacted to the pressures of grown-up life. The usual, regular thing, so we innocently supposed, was to be in the Cabinet or on the Opposition Front Bench, or in general to be some sort of an eminence.[1]

In other words, John Strachey could hardly avoid the expectation that he would be at the centre of things, and this was undoubtedly to affect his involvement in the labour movement.

The specifically political education that he received from his family was in keeping with this general atmosphere. St Loe may have been a political maverick, as between the Liberal and Conservative Parties, but his attitude to the Left was very clear. In 1908 he wrote *The Problems and Perils of Socialism*, in which he warned the 'working man' that socialism was disastrous because it would destroy self-interest, the motive-force to the production of wealth, and would then need to introduce compulsion, which would lead to slave labour, waste and inefficiency. If he was subsequently to become a little more open-minded about the Labour Party, his position did not shift substantially and he regarded Mussolini as 'a great man' when he met him in 1924.[2] In addition, he was an extreme patriot, who had established a rifle club and military training in 1906 in case Britain became involved in war and, during the war itself, he was totally opposed to conscientious objectors. John Strachey's mother, Amy, shared her husband's views but was less of an influence over John's opinions. This was largely becuase she had never recovered from the death of his elder brother, and consequently devoted little time to him – a fact which, no doubt, added to his emotional difficulties in later life.

There were few outward signs that John Strachey would rebel against his background. At Eton he participated – apparently willingly – in all the normal activities, including the Army corps, and was greatly influenced by his extremely right-wing history teacher. At Oxford he not only became involved in debating, acting and writing plays and poetry but also edited a Conservative journal with his life-long friend, Robert Boothby. And in 1922, when he left university without graduating (because he was seriously ill with pneumonia), he joined the *Spectator* in the general expectation that he would take it over from St Loe.

The first stage in his apparently sudden shift to the Left had probably come with his loss of religious belief while at Oxford. According to his later account, he became conscious of the break-up of the old world: – 'by a sudden and bewildering loss of faith in the whole moral, religious and social ideology which we had inherited'. This led to a rejection of 'that whole unparalleled structure of repressions and taboos' which constituted the 'religious and moral superstructure of British upper class life'.[3]

The more specific catalysts for his adoption of a radical perspective were probably affairs with two women. The first, which began in 1922, was with a married French woman, Yvette Fouquet. Although she was not a socialist, she was radical, free-thinking, extremely knowledgeable about literature and cosmopolitan in outlook. The attack on conventional morality which the affair involved and Yvette's general cultural and political attitudes led him to question much about himself. As he told her: 'It was your effort to break up the vileness of my British bourgeoisdom that gave me a chance.'[4] The second affair had more obvious political relevance, in the narrow sense, for it was with Elizabeth Ponsonby, daughter of Arthur Ponsonby, shortly to be a minister in the first Labour government. This led to a new circle of acquaintances. Arthur Ponsonby subsequently introduced Strachey to Fenner Brockway of the Independent Labour Party (ILP), who gave him some work in the ILP information department and 'finding that he had a clear, persuasive style of writing' invited him to do some writing for the *New Leader*.[5] By the end of 1923 or beginning of 1924 Strachey had become a socialist and joined the ILP.

Of course these encounters would not have led to his conversion unless he had had some predisposition towards the Left. This had already been revealed in the liberal form of conservatism that he had espoused at Oxford, where he had also been influenced on foreign policy issues by E. D. Morel of the Union for Democratic Control. Nevertheless, Strachey himself obviously believed that his socialist beliefs had come about through 'accidental' factors:

> It is impossible for anyone from the middle and upper classes to conceive of Socialism by reading books, or from any form of external contact. The only way that such a person can come to it is by accident. What usually happens is that somebody who is maladjusted to his own class, sooner or later quarrels with existing society on some issue which has nothing to do with Socialism and so comes right into the other world. Then, when he comes into contact with Socialists and Socialism from the inside, he will begin to get a real conception of the new point of view.[6]

In Strachey's own case, the 'quarrel' was probably the affair with

The making of a socialist

Yvette, but the 'mal-adjustment to his own class' was more complex. His relationship with his mother was distant; he had been unhappy at Eton; and had ultimately found Oxford trivial. His dark, Mediterranean appearance made him look very different from the more typical 'White Anglo-Saxon Protestants' of the British upper classes; he found the social conventions and conforming pressures of his life-style stifling; and, above all, he was extremely intellectual, with a passion for ideas. All this made him an 'outsider' in his own class. Despite a rather cold exterior, he was also extremely emotional. Once his underlying unhappiness about his role in society was brought to the surface, the strength of his feelings indeed carried him 'right into the other world'. For Strachey was someone whose commitment was always total.

When he joined the ILP, Fenner Brockway found him 'sincere in his desire to help the Socialist Movement, but knowing very little about it'.[7] This may have been so, but he was already reading widely and would soon show his theoretical grasp and writing ability. Nor, given his background, was he content to remain a rank-and-file member. Instead, he decided to make a political career in the labour movement and sought adoption as a parliamentary condidate. The contemporary Labour Party was so over-eager to attract middle-class enthusiasts that he was immediately offered a potentially winnable seat in Birmingham Aston, where he stood for the first time (unsuccessfully) in October 1924.

The Labour Party had thus gained an extraordinarily energetic and intelligent upper-class recruit. He was certainly also ambitious, but it would be quite wrong to regard him as a careerist: with his background, connections and abilities Strachey could have succeeded in any political movement, or in journalism or academia. The problem was not ambition itself, but that his upbringing, character and talents would make him extremely impatient when the Labour Party proved unresponsive to new ideas. It would probably have been better had he been required to work at grass-roots level for some years before being offered a parliamentary seat, but that was the fault of the party rather than of Strachey himself.

When he first stood for Birmingham Aston, Ramsay MacDonald's first minority Labour government had just been chased out of power by a dishonest, Tory-inspired, anti-Communist scare. But it would be difficult to regard the administration as a success in any case. It is true that its independence was limited (given the need for Liberal support in Parliament), that its opponents were particularly malevolent in their propaganda and that it held office for only ten months. But John Wheatley, the ILP Clydesider who was Housing Minister, was probably the only member of the government who improved the life-chances of workers (by stimulating council house construction). Otherwise, it made no impact upon the problems facing the working class, despite the expectations which had been raised. In particular, unemployment remained at approximately 10 per cent, the traditional export industries continued to stagnate and there was widspread poverty in many parts of the country.

For the moment, none of this dented Strachey's enthusiasm. In October 1924, he thus proclaimed that, if the Labour party had faults:

> they will be the faults of youth... not the dull, irrevocable errors of the senility of an institution. [It is]... the one party which has the three most important possessions that a political party can desire – *a cause to fight for, a leader who can inspire, and a deeply enthusiastic rank and file to follow and support him.*[8] [original emphasis]

This revealed the emotional and idealistic side of Strachey's socialism, but his theoretical approach was soon to become evident.

Strachey's most sustained interest over the next thirty years was to be in 'political economy' – the interaction between politics and economics. This was not because he believed that the development of the economy was an end in itself. On the contrary, he was most interested in the full development of culture and society, or 'civilisation' as he often called it. However, he believed that this was unattainable without a firm economic base and thus saw the establishment of economic 'health' as the prerequisite for social and cultural well-being. Since he was to regard the economy as fundamentally unsound for most of his life, his immediate preoccupation was to seek the resolution of the problems by the appropriate political and economic measures.

He had no formal training in economics but was attracted to the subject through the influence of his father (and perhaps to find a link with his mother through her famous ancestor, Nassau Senior). One of his first tasks on leaving Oxford had been to collaborate with Boothby in editing St Loe Strachey's economic writings, and through this he had become aware of the current controversies. His father had also introduced him to Keynes, who clearly influenced his thinking at this stage. Meanwhile, his conversion to the Left led him to socialist economic theory and, by September 1924, he had become convinced that Marx's insight into capitalism was fundamentally correct, and that it was he who had 'started economics as a science'.[9] Strachey's opportunity to combine his interest in economic theory with socialist politics came with his adoption as a parliamentary candidate in Birmingham, for it was here that he began his collaboration with Sir Oswald Mosley, who was also nursing a constituency there.

By October 1924 Mosley was already well known – or even notorious – as a renegade MP who had been elected as a Conservative MP in 1918 and had defected to the Labour Party in March 1924. He was soon impatient with the timidity of the leadership on the burning issue of unemployment and was convinced that there was a possible solution in an expansionist economic policy. Strachey readily agreed, and the two worked closely to elaborate the so-called 'Birmingham proposals', which were adopted by the local ILP and Labour Party in the summer of 1925. Mosley was more experienced, slightly older and more charismatic than Strachey, and thus played the major role in securing local support for the proposals. Mosley was also the dominant personality within the partnership, but it is far less clear who was the major intellectual influence. Mosley tended to take the credit himself and wrote the proposals up in a short pamphlet, *Revolution by Reason*. Strachey then reinforced this impression by attributing the ideas to Mosley and dedicating his first book, of the same title, 'To O.M., who may some day do the things of which we dream.'[10] However, the intellectual relationship was probably far more complex than this implies. Mosley no doubt provided the impetus, but it was Strachey who provided the real exposition and theoretical underpinning for the proposals and was able to place them in a long-term context. Both this and his later preoccupation with socialist economic theory suggest that he played a crucial role in the formulation and development of the doctrine. Furthermore, there were differences in emphasis between the two versions and, although both were nationalistic, Mosley's was overtly racist in one passage and full of declamatory rhetoric. Such differences, foreshadowing their political separation six years later, imply that Strachey was more independent than is often argued.

As Strachey surveyed the situation from the Midlands with Mosley in 1925, two points seemed evident: first, that British capitalism was a declining economic system; and secondly, that the Labour government had neither implemented the necessary measures to reverse the decline nor had even really understood the problems. For Strachey, both failings represented a crisis of immense magnitude. Not only was he moved by the scale of human suffering caused by poverty and unemployment but he also believed that it could lead to something he viewed with horror – violent revolution. It was, therefore, imperative to find an alternative rather than allowing a 'blind, head-on collision' between workers and capitalists to lead to an 'abyss of chaos, social regression and catastrophe'.[11] A 'revolution by reason' was thus needed to prevent unchecked class conflict bringing about a 'dark age of unreason'.

Strachey and Mosley were quite justified in their conviction that dominant opinion in the Labour Party (let alone the pro-capitalist parties) was incapable of finding a solution to the economic problems because it was wedded to anachronistic orthodoxies. The Birmingham proposals therefore represented an attempt to convert the Labour leadership to an alternative strategy.

The current pro-capitalist conventional wisdom, which Mosley and Strachey were challenging, was that the economic malaise would be cured if the pre-1914 world could be restored. In reality, this had gone for ever. The first World War had ended British pre-eminence in the international economic and financial system; and the pattern of international trade and payments had itself been undermined both by the war and by the instability of the subsequent peace settlement. Nevertheless, the general assumption was that a return to 'normality' in domestic and international markets would restore the British economy to its 'equilibrium' level. At home, this meant that the government's major economic role should be confined to balancing its budget, while the restoration of the Gold Standard was seen as the way to guarantee a stable system of international payments. (The Conservative government thus returned to the Gold Standard, with sterling at its pre-war parity, in 1925.)

In fact, all these measures exacerbated the stagnation of the British economy. Since producers for the domestic market were suffering from falling prices and low demand, the attempt to balance the budget tended to mean a reduction of expenditure as revenue from tax receipts fell. But this then led to a further slow-down in total economic activity. Restoration of the Gold Stardard was to reinforce the deflationary pressures: since sterling was now to be overvalued by about 10 per cent, exporters would try to reduce their costs by an equivalent amount in order to restore their international competitiveness. This meant further pressure on wages and employment and a generally stagnant economy.

Naturally, the Labour Party was bitterly opposed to poverty and unemployment, justifiably attributing these ills to capitalism. But while socialism was proclaimed as the solution, Labour was a gradualist party and therefore needed palliatives if it was going to bring about improvements in working-class living standards and so fulfil its *raison d'être*. And it was in this respect that it had failed most dismally to escape from current economic and financial orthodoxy. For example, while the 1924 Labour government had wanted to improve conditions for the unemployed, it had possessed no distinct national economic strategy to increase employment, and its acceptance of Treasury orthodoxy about balanced budgets prevented it from even giving adequate relief to those currently enemployed.

Strachey and Mosley were therefore attempting to counter deeply engrained assumptions when proposing a new policy for economic regeneration. Moreover, they were not only challenging the programme of the Labour leadership but were also questioning traditional socialist remedies. Because they wanted a strategy which would have immmediate results, they rejected both Marxism and Fabianism as a basis for their proposals. Strachey accepted Marxist theory as providing a valid long-term insight into the internal contradictions of capitalism. But he quoted with approval Keynes's famous dictum that 'in the long run we shall

all be dead' and stressed the need for short-term measures. He was still more dismissive of the Fabian rationale of 'the inevitability of gradualness', arguing that it was too gradual, and that there was nothing inevitable about it. He also criticised the more specific Fabian and Labour Party panacea of piecemeal nationalisation, claiming that it was useless to suppose that the world would be transformed by leaving a socialist government to deal with some depressed and obsolete industries, while capitalists gaily re-invested in new fields. The Strachey–Mosley aim was to formulate measures which would make the maximum immediate impact on the economy *as a whole* so as to stimulate production and transfer resources to the working-class. Their belief was that this could be achieved by a synthesis of two existing critiques of orthodoxy.

One part of their programme stemmed from the notion of 'under-consumption'. This was particularly associated with the radical-liberal, John Hobson, whose pre-war writing had been used by Lenin in the development of his theory of imperialism. Hobson was now close to the ILP and was, in fact, to play a leading role in devising the economic policy which that party was to adopt in 1926 in preference to the Strachey–Mosley proposals.

According to Hobson, 'under-consumption' was the fundamental economic problem and redistribution was the solution. The basic argument was that there was insufficient effective demand in the economy because the rich could not buy more than a limited amount of the goods produced, as their needs were sated, while the poor could not do so because they lacked the necessary purchasing power. Redistribution would therefore increase total effective demand and thereby enable manufacturers to produce at full capacity. Utilisation of full capacity would simultaneously increase the size of the work-force required and thus also cure the unemployment problem.

Strachey accepted this at general level, but argued that it ignored a vital factor in the situation: the problem of falling prices. Influenced by Keynes's recent work on money and price levels in *A Tract on Monetary Reform*, he argued that manufacturers would have no incentive to produce more (even to meet increasing demand) unless they could be sure that price levels would not fall further. Otherwise, any increase in output would lead to falling profit margins and perhaps a decline in total profits. Keynes also believed that there was a close relationship between the amount of money in circulation and price levels. This meant that prices would actually fall if more commodities were produced unless the amount of money in circulation was also increased. Strachey and Mosley accepted this argument and, therefore, believed that it would be insufficient simply to increase demand in the economy by redistribution to the poor. It was also necessary to regulate the money supply so that an increase in production could be realised without a fall in prices. This involved total opposition to the return to the Gold Standard, for this related the money supply (and therefore also prices) to gold reserves rather than production. Strachey (though not Keynes) also argued that a second essential requirement was the nationalisation of the Bank of England so that the profits sought by financial interests would not impede the co-ordination between banking and production.

If the more socialistic 'under-consumption' theory needed to be complemented by Keynes's monetary theory, Strachey was equally adamant that the latter alone would be inedaquate. Increasing the supply of money might simply lead to greater inflation, which would add to the maldistribution of wealth by benefiting traders and speculators at the expense of the masses. This, he believed, led straight back to a socialist prescription and showed that without redistribution of ownership 'the ills from which we suffer are incurable'.[12]

The making of a socialist

The 'Birmingham proposals' thus envisaged the creation:

> of (*i*) a public banking system capable of giving such accommodation to industry as will enable it to increase the purchasing power of the workers, so that a new home market can absorb industry's real productive capacity; and (*ii*) of an Economic Council for the co-ordination and control of that productive capacity. These institutions give a Labour Government control of the economic system.[13]

The functions of the Economic Council would be to create and maintain new effective demand by forcing up wages and the unemployment benefits of the working classes. It would also secure better organisation and planning of national production and distribution, so that the new demand led to an increase in goods and services rather than an increase in prices. The public banking and credit system would be able to pay higher wages out of the pooled credit resources of the country (based on the knowledge that further production was to be forthcoming). It could also subsidise those manufacturers who could not afford higher wages, while simultaneously subjecting them to greater control by the Economic Council. But there would also need to be heavy direct taxation on large incomes so that purchasing power could be transferred to the working classes, which also meant an increased demand for necessities at the expense of luxury goods. Overall, it was thus argued that monetary expansion, coupled with a comprehensive policy of socialist reorganisation, could lead to a continuous and steady increase in production.

As contemporary critics pointd out, there were weaknesses in the proposals themselves and in Strachey's exposition of them. They were inadequate on the international side and, in particular, failed to face the fact that it was traditional export industries (coal, steel and textiles) which were stagnating rather than those producing for working-class consumption. This meant that there were difficulties in the whole notion of 'under-consumption'

13

unless accompanied by a really fundamental change in the pattern of production. Nor was the relationship between the money supply and price levels as close as Strachey believed: indeed the money supply was neither as fundamental nor as autonomous as he suggested. There would also be vast practical problems in co-ordinating the money supply, production and demand as he envisaged. As Hugh Dalton, the emergent economic brain of the Labour leadership, put it: the proposed Economic Council would have so many tasks that he could not 'see the necessary supermen on the horizon who could tackle them all'.[14] And if these were the criticisms of conventional economists, Mosley and Strachey were simultaneously attacked from the Left for tinkering with capitalism instead of overthrowing it.

Yet Mosley and Strachey were making a real effort to formulate an economic policy which would address the fundamental problems which would confront the next Labour government. The attempt to understand the relationship between the banking system and the economy as a whole was both important and unusual on the Left as, indeed, was the overall endeavour to provide a synthesis between socialist and non-socialist economic theory. The attempt to formulate measures which would make the maximum immediate impact on the economy *as a whole* was also an advance on Fabian gradualism and the common tendency to view nationalisation *per se* as the solution, and to minimise the problems of production. In contrast, many of their critics were content to reiterate existing orthodoxies camouflaged with socialist rhetoric. Even Hugh Dalton, who made some cogent criticisms of Strachey's book, appeared complacent about the major problems of the day, and there was never any chance that the party leadership would adopt the 'Birmingham proposals'.

In fact *Revolution by Reason* was not taken up by the ILP either, which adopted the so-called *Living Wage* proposals instead. But this was not because the ILP was too cautious. *The Living Wage*, which was devised primarily by Hobson himself and another major ILP thinker, H. N. Brailsford, was at least as radical and innovative as the Strachey–Mosley proposals, and was wider in range. It was adopted in preference to the Birmingham Programme because it was the product of a study group which had been specifically established to advise the ILP on economic strategy. The main differences were in its greater emphasis on under-consumption (for which a minimum wage was seen as a principal remedy), and nationalisation and in placing much less stress on monetary policy than the 'Birmingham proposals'. Strachey criticised *The Living Wage* for its failure in this respect and argued that, without such a policy, there was no way to 'break through the vicious circle of poverty and unemployment'.[15]

However, the Hobson–Strachey dispute was really within a shared framework, for there was far more similarity between the two than between either of them and the Labour leadership. The tragedy was that *The Living Wage* made no impact at all on key figures in the trade union movement, who feared that it would interfere with collective wage bargaining, or with the Labour leadership. Indeed the ILP lost all its remaining influence over Ramsay MacDonald after late 1925, when it moved to the Left and became more overtly critical of the Labour leader (see further discussion below). He reciprocated by dismissing the ILP's economic ideas as 'flashy futilities'.[16] Instead the Labour Party leadership maintained its commitment to financial and economic orthodoxy – the policy that was to lead to disaster in 1931.

Despite the limited impact of *Revolution by Reason*, Strachey's role in the formulation and exposition of the 'Birmingham proposals' was already giving him greater prominence in the Labour movement. The ability of a twenty-four-year-old, untrained in economics, to explain and synthesise differing theories was remarkable, and did not go unnoticed. Even Dalton, who disagreed with Keynes and detested Mosley, thought that

Strachey had written 'a vital and stimulating book'.[17]; and MacDonald, who probably did not understand the theory, wrote him a friendly note about it. More concretely, as a result of a change in leadership, Strachey was now to achieve an important position in the ILP.

For some time there had been tension between the leader of the ILP, Clifford Allen, who offered critical support to the Labour Party leadership, and more militant members, particularly in the Clydeside. The failure of the Labour government had brought matters to a head and in Ocotber 1925 one of the Clydesiders, James Maxton, became leader and the party adopted a more assertive, left-wing stance. In fact, the problems of the ILP were legion, for there was no organisational unity or discipline over its MPs, and key personnel in the parliamentary Labour Party leadership, including Snowden and MacDonald, remained ILP members. Most fundamental of all, its long-term future was threatened by the 1918 constitution of the Labour Party which, for the first time, allowed individual Labour Party membership on a constituency party basis. Previously, the ILP had been the main focus for constituency activity, and the change naturally undermined its vitality and role. These cumulative pressures, and the effects of being 'squeezed' between the Communist Party and Labour after 1932, were eventually to eliminate the ILP as a significant political force. However, this rapid decline was not yet obvious in 1925 as Maxton tried to regenerate the organisation on a left-wing programme and establish greater control over ILP MPs.

In these circumstances a new editor for the ILP monthly, *Socialist Review*, was needed, rather than allowing Ramsay MacDonald to take back the editorship as Clifford Allen had wanted. Strachey had demonstrated his writing skill and ability in socialist theory. Given his experience on the *Spectator*, he was the ideal choice and took up the new position in time to produce his first edition in February 1926.

There is no doubt that the journal was given a new lease of life under Strachey's editorship for he made the issues far more lively, covering almost all areas of interest to socialists, and attracted a wide range of contributors. He also wrote an editorial (and sometimes an article) in almost every issue, discussing current events and theories in a stimulating and often humorous way. The writing style which was to make his books so influential in the 1930s now became apparent.

The first issue of *Socialist Review* edited by Strachey was in harmony with Maxton's line as leader of the ILP, for it boldly proclaimed:

> To those forces, both powerful and insidious, which seek to turn Labour from its purpose, to water down its drastic proposals, to blunt the aggressive spirit of its leader, the Independent Labour Party, and the Socialist Review offer. . .uncompromising resistance.[18]

In fact, Strachey was far less militant than this implied, for he had not abandoned the peaceful constitutionalism which had provided the political rationale for the 'Birmingham proposals'. However, during the final stages of writing *Revolution by Reason* and in the early months of editing *Socialist Review*, Strachey was preoccupied by the threat of a general strike.

This would take place if the coal-owners carried out their threat of implementing wage-cuts and lock-outs on the miners, for the TUC was pledged to call out virtually all trade unionists in this event. In 1925 the conflict had been averted by a temporary state subsidy to the industry, but this was due to end in May 1926 and the government was simply buying time to make the necessary preparations to defeat the strike when it came. Strachey made it clear that:

> if our rulers, in the mad panic of threatened privilege, precipitate an industrial catastrophe, we shall be free, in heart and in conscience,

to uphold the working people of our country with unquestioning devotion and irresistible determination.[19]

But it was quite apparent that he would regard this as a disaster and yearned for a rational alternative compatible with peaceful constitutional change. When the General Strike finally came, Strachey ended months of open agonising on the issue and participated in mass working-class politics for the first time.

The General Strike of May 1926 was of crucial significance in the history of the British labour movement. Faced with the government's total determination to defeat the trade union movement, the Labour Party leadership distanced itself from the strikers, and the TUC backed down after eight days, without securing any of its demands. The miners were betrayed – finally forced to capitulate months later – and the organised working-class movement was gravely weakened. Trade union membership declined and its powers were restricted in the Trade Disputes Act in 1927. The union leadership was soon putting all its faith in the Parliamentary Labour Party (PLP) and in collaboration with industrialists over the economy and working conditions (in the so-called Mond–Turner talks, which the TUC and leading employers began in 1928).

The experience of the General Strike was also to be highly significant in Strachey's own political development. In the short term he entered the fray by editing the strike bulletin on behalf of the Birmingham Trade Union Emergency Committee, leading to his arrest for incitement to disaffection for an article claiming that troops were defecting to the side of the workers. Whereas he had previously feared such an upsurge of class revolt as presaging the collapse of civilisation, he now found it an exhilarating experience of solidarity and comradeship. This did not mean that he immediately sided with the opponents of the Labour and trade union leadership, but there were soon signs that he found

The making of a socialist

the drive and energy of the mass strike a refreshing contrast with the cautious constitutionalism of the PLP. This was reinforced by his commitment to the miners' cause, which continued long after the strike was called off, for Strachey now also began to edit the *Miner* on behalf of the Miners Federation. This brought him into far more direct contact with working-class activists and, in particular, with A. J.Cook, the miners' leader.

Strachey's close association and friendship with Cook, with whom he travelled to the Soviet Union as a guest of Soviet miners in 1928, had a major impact on his views and led him towards a much more radical political perspective. This was reinforced by an increasing interest in, and acceptance, of Marxism. The emotional catalyst of the General Strike was thus now followed by a development in Strachey's theoretical stance which was to lead him away from the perspective elaborated in *Revolution by Reason*.

By 1928 he used a Marxist framework to attack the position that he himself had previously held. Announcing that he used to be a 'currency crank', he claimed that:

> the fundamental error of the currency crank is taking the money shortage for a cause instead of symptom.
>
> The perpetual under-issue of the means of payment, which is a chronic feature of modern capitalism, is no accident due to some muddle on the part of the bankers. It is an integral and absolutely essential part of modern capitalism, and it is impossible to abolish it without abolishing capitalism as a whole. To think as I used to think, that one could have a scientific socialised banking system, pursuing a rational, scientific currency policy, whilst leaving the rest of capitalism and class domination intact, is mere Utopianism.

In reality, the 'currency crank' was asking for the rich to consent 'to the complete drying up of the present source of their unearned income!'

> No wonder that the banker's answer is merely a smile, or, if he is

in a very good temper, perhaps a wink.[20]

And the next month he stated quite explicitly, that 'Marxian terminology is by far the best method of discussing modern political problems.'[21]

The shift in his explanatory framework was coupled with a far more critical attitude to both the Labour Party and the ILP as political agencies for change. By the end of 1927 he was hoping that all those who were not really left-wing would resign from the ILP and he called for a far more comprehensive, militant policy. Emulating Communist doctrine, he claimed that any party which knew what was happening to British capitalism should be able to define the correct attitude for workers to take. A remodelled ILP should do this and, still more important, should act as a check on the inevitable tendency of the Labour Party leadership 'to go to sleep'.

Naturally, none of this was popular with the Labour Party leadership and, as early as February 1927, Ramsay MacDonald ceased his monthly column for *Socialist Review*. But nor was Strachey unreservedly on the side of the ILP Left, as was shown by his attitude to the so-called 'Cook–Maxton Manifesto'.

In June 1928 James Maxton and A. J. Cook issued a manifesto addressed to 'the workers of Britain'. This was an attempt to build a militant rank-and-file movement against 'class-collaboration', epitomised by the Mond–Turner talks between the TUC and employers. Strachey welcomed the political purposes of the manifesto and hoped that it would lead more non-socialists to leave the ILP. But he was very critical of its economic ideas and thought it was naive to believe that a potentially revolutionary programme could be introduced through Parliament. In fact, Strachey's political position was, at this stage, convoluted for he was simultaneously attracted and repelled by the Communist Party (CP) and by the revolutionary implications of Marxist theory.

In the immediate aftermath of the General Strike the CP's membership had shot up from 6,000 to 10,730, with the majority of new members being miners. Both because of his work on the *Miner* and his interest in Marxism, he turned his attention to this apparently growing movement.

He admired the CP's organisational ability and discipline, believing that these compared very favourably with the Labour Party and the ILP. He was also impressed by its emphasis on theory, and particularly by the work of R. Palme Dutt, the CP's main theoretician and a central figure in its leadership. Thus, when Dutt produced a critique of ILP policy, *Socialism and the Living Wage* (1927), which, amongst other things, refuted his own ideas, Strachey termed it 'a very great achievement' and regretted the fact that the rest of the labour movement was not producing such 'excellent' work.[22] In comparison with CP theory, he now saw even ILP left-wing statements as a 'little amateurish', while the Labour Party was 'theoretically barren'. These favourable attitudes to the CP were coupled with an increasingly positive appraisal of both the Russian Revolution and the contemporary Soviet Union, particularly after his visit there in 1928.

But his condemnation of Communism was at least as strong. This was partly because he believed that the CP had 'completely and utterly cut itself off from the British masses', who regarded 'Communists as doctrinaires preaching an utterly unintelligible creed in a jargon divorced from all reality'.[23] He found the CP too dogmatic in both its general stance and its underlying theory. He thus saw the typical Communist as unreceptive to new ideas and 'so absorbed in the battle that he forgets what he is fighting for'.[24] Moreover, although he became convinced of the general superiority of Communist economic analysis, he did not believe that it was infallible. Since the CP, in line with the Communist International, adopted an increasingly 'ultra-left' sectarian line from the beginning of 1928, Strachey also believed that its policy would be disastrous if its predictions proved wrong. For it was now denouncing all non-Communist socialists and shunning any co-operation with organisations like the ILP on the assumption that a revolutionary situation was developing with the imminent collapse of capitalism. Strachey was not convinced of the immediacy of the downfall of the economic system and thought that the working classes would be in a dangerously isolated position, unable to secure any reforms, if they followed the CP line. Indeed, by late 1928, he had come to believe that the economy had entered a phase of stabilisation and this made him still more opposed to current CP policy.

Thus he grew dissatisfied with all the available party positions – ILP, Labour Party and CP. His own position was highly individual. He was fascinated by revolutionary Marxism but could not accept it in what he understood to be its orthodox form. In particular, he believed it too deterministic, with an over-emphasis on economic factors. He felt that individuals could be 'unfree', even if they were satisfied in material terms, and he therefore thought that socialist theory should include psychology, which it tended to ignore. Nevertheless, while arguing that socialist theory should not be 'scholastically rigid', he saw the works of Marx, Lenin and Engels as essential.[25] However, he was also convinced that the situation in Britain was not 'revolutionary'. In late 1928, he speculated as to the real needs of the moment and the implications for a party programme.

His starting point was an absolute requirement that the movement must not cut itself off from the working class. He was therefore totally opposed to the CP, which was now in decline as a result of its sectarian policy, and to the suggestion that the ILP should disaffiliate from the Labour Party. The task was to devise a programme which would educate the workers to show them that they could get nothing from capitalism except as an organised army pressing forward to complete domination. This would warn them that:

> the best they could hope for in the next two or three years was a Labour Government which would have to rule largely at the mercy of the capitalist classes in the country. Such a programme would point out the narrow limits of effective action that such a government could undertake, but it would point out that it could secure certain things, some of which would be of definite material benefit to the workers . . . and some of which . . . would be of the greatest assistance to the workers in their further struggle.[26]

Such a programme should explain (without using the term itself) that Britain was a 'capitalist dictatorship' and that in the present world situation there was little chance of establishing working-class power. The task of a Labour government would be to strengthen the power of workers within the existing system, to relieve poverty and – most difficult – to encroach on the economic bastions of capitalism, particularly by nationalising the Bank of England and establishing credit control. Nothing more was possible until the workers were ready to take power and create a classless society: 'Therefore while the programme would dispel the pacifist delusions of the workers, it would warn them against hopeless insurrectionism.' As he campaigned for his own election and that of the Labour Party as a whole in May 1929, he became still more convinced that Britain had entered a period of capitalist stabilisation and that the best way in which socialists could utilise this situation was by analysing the drifts and drives of world capitalism and establishing a solid platform of theory. Socialists who remained within the Labour Party should work for immediate reforms of benefit to the workers, and attempt to keep a hard core of real socialist opinion alive within the party so as to prevent its degeneration into a 'mere Liberal Party'. They must prepare themselves for the crisis which would recur.[27]

John Strachey

Apart from the fact that he was soon to be proved quite wrong about the stabilisation of capitalism, what are we to make of Strachey's political position as he sought election as a Labour MP in May 1929? He obviously retained few illusions about a Labour government introducing a 'new Jerusalem' and was certainly nearer to Marxism than the overwhelming majority of parliamentary Labour candidates. But if his overall political position was tortuous, this was not just because of the difficulties of reconciling revolutionary Marxism to a non-revolutionary situation. It was also related to contradictions within his own character and position.

Strachey was, as already noted, always emotional as well as theoretical in his outlook. But at this stage, the two aspects were not properly integrated. For example, while many of his criticisms of CP dogmatism and sectarianism were valid, Strachey's attitude was probably influenced as much by emotional as theoretical considerations. As a member of the British upper classes, he was alienated by the apparent class hatred of the CP. After all, Boothby, who was now a Conservative MP, remained his closest friend, and Strachey had not broken away from his own family. He could, thus, accept Marxism as a *theory* and could advocate a militant form of socialism, but was unable to accept the total change in his life-style – emotional as well as material – that Communism seemed to imply. Indeed, the contradictions in his emotional and theoretical life multiplied in 1929 when he married an American heiress, Esther Murphy.

In purely theoretical terms, he now saw a form of Marxism as the only coherent perspective for a socialist. However, his emotional life remained separate as he looked forward to a new and exciting career as a Labour MP. Moreover, his theory was perhaps influenced by his emotions as he no doubt wished (consciously or unconsciously) to believe that capitalism had stabilised and that reform rather than revolution was on the political agenda.

These contradictions were epitomised in his election campaign, which showed no traces of Marxist analysis and included an appeal by his highly Conservative mother to support her son as someone who would 'do his best for everyone'.[28] It is this lack of integration between theory and emotions which does much to explain the surprising role which Strachey was to play once the Labour Party was elected to government.

2 In and out of the New Party (1929–1931)

In the General Election of May 1929 Labour emerged as the biggest single party, with 287 MPs, compared with 260 for the Conservatives. Ramsay MacDonald was able to form only a minority government, but this time Labour appeared to be in a stronger position than in 1924, as the Liberals were reduced to only fifty-nine seats. The stagnating economy, with unemployment at 1,164,000 in June 1929, was once again the major problem facing the new government, but there did appear to be some prospect of improvement with the relative stabilisation of the international economic and political situation in the late 1920s.

Just over two years later, in August 1931, the Labour government was to collapse in ignominious failure, in the midst of the world economic crisis. By then unemployment was over 2,800,000 and still rising; the volume of exports had declined by 40 per cent since 1929, while imports remained constant. In the ensuing currency crisis, the Labour cabinet accepted, by eleven votes to nine, a package of public expenditure reductions, including a cut of 10 per cent in unemployment benefit. The close vote provided too small a majority to provide the political stability required to secure a loan from American and French bankers, and the whole government was expected to resign. However, MacDonald accepted the blandishments of the King and the leaders of the opposition parties and, on 24 August 1931, agreed to lead a National government. Three other Labour ministers joined MacDonald, but the Labour Party as a whole went into opposition and the National government was to be dominated by the Conservative Party.

The failure of the second Labour government was to create a political trauma for the Left which had ramifications far beyond the immediate events. For, in the context of the worldwide crisis of capitalism and the development of Fascism, it was to raise an obvious question: was peaceful, evolutionary change possible, or were the only alternatives Fascism or Communism? No-one would put this question with greater clarity or answer it with greater force than John Strachey. However, he was only to do so *after* August 1931. Before then he experienced his own political and personal crisis. In February 1931 he had joined Sir Oswald Mosley in forming the New Party – a movement from which the British Union of Fascists (BUF) was to develop the next year. Although he withdrew long before the formation of the BUF, there was no sharp and total break between the two movements. Strachey himself was, therefore, well aware that he had pulled back from the brink of embracing Fascism as a solution to the crisis.

Strachey's five-month excursion into the New Party, followed by his break from Mosley whom he then passionately denounced as a Fascist, can be explained only by his own history between 1929 and 1931 in the context of the failure of the Labour government.

In May 1929 Strachey had every reason for feeling optimistic. He had defeated his Conservative opponent in Aston and was immediately rewarded by becoming parliamentary private secretary to Mosley, who had been appointed Chancellor of the Duchy of Lancaster to help co-ordinate Labour's policy on unemployment. Since he also believed that the government had scope to make valuable reforms, he felt that he would be able to work with Mosley to make the kind of impact that they had originally hoped to have with their 1925 'Birmingham proposals'. Strachey therefore expressed full confidence in MacDonald's administration and criticised those who attacked it from the Left without giving it a chance. However, by the autumn his early confidence had evaporated and he was beginning to attack the government as openly as was consistent wth his position as a parliamentary private secretary. The speed with which this change in attitude occurred can be explained on two levels: first, his own character and the nature of his relationship with Mosley; and secondly, a justifiable exasperation with government policy. These can be considered in turn, although they obviously operated simultaneously.

There were some major differences between Strachey and Mosley: while Strachey was attracted to Marxism and the Soviet Union, Mosley preferred American mass-market capitalism; while Strachey was a theoretician who did not take decisions easily, Mosley was decisive, self-confident and ambitious for personal power. However, such differences were obscured by the many similarities between the two. Both were upper class; both thought they understood the needs of the time and were impatient with those who put obstacles in their way; both thought the young had greater insight than the old; and both believed that the immediate solution to Britain's unemployment problem lay in an interventionist reflationary policy. All this united them and had led to a close personal friendship so that, for example, Mosley had acted as best man at Strachey's wedding in April 1929. Above all it led them to act as a team within the government, with which they would grow frustrated very quickly. However, this tendency was greatly reinforced by the objective circumstances in which they were placed.

Both the structure of decision-making on unemployment and the prevailing policy were bound to antagonise anyone who saw the solution to the problem in expansionist terms. Mosley was not in the cabinet but had to report to J. H. Thomas, the Lord

Privy Seal, who had overall responsibility for unemployment policy. Thomas was a right-wing trade unionist, with no clear economic ideas, who was jealous of his own position and extremely wary of radical ideas. Mosley was, therefore, unable to win his support and, by autumn 1929, Thomas's main initiative had been a wholly irrelevant trip to Canada to try to increase exports and encourage emigration. In fact, it is unlikely that Mosley would have made a great deal of headway even if Thomas had been more sympathetic, since Philip Snowden, the Chancellor of the Exchequer, dominated economic policy and was as wedded to orthodoxy as in 1924. Nevertheless, the fact that Thomas did not even put pressure on the restrictive Treasury viewpoint would have made Mosley's situation an unenviable one for anyone who wanted to introduce a radical strategy.

At the beginning of October Strachey therefore sounded the first public warning about the position, arguing that the government could not survive unless it soon found a solution to the problem of unemployment. He made three criticisms of the government's efforts: (1) that the existing structure of government wasted the abilities of the three ministers under Thomas; (2) that the cabinet wrongly favoured unemployment relief at the expense of constructive projects which might create further employment, and ignored the inhibiting effect of the high bank rate; and (3) that it was overrating the economic difficulties involved in overcoming the problems, and was hesitant in grappling with them over a wide front.[1] This article had almost certainly been agreed in advance with Mosley, who was, at this stage, prevented by his position from publicly voicing any criticism of the government.

Almost immediately after this warning to the government, the Wall Street Crash unleashed the world depression. Although Strachey did not recognise the gravity of the situation (still clinging to his view that capitalism had stabilised), it soon became clear that unemployment was increasing rather than diminishing. This gave added urgency to the attempt to counter the government's passive policy and, by December, work began on the alternative proposals which were soon to become known as the 'Mosley Memorandum'. Strachey was in the USA during the final drafting but, according to Boothby (who was friendly with both men at the time), he was a major influence.

The memorandum addressed both political and economic issues.[2] It began with new proposals for the machinery of government, advocating a powerful executive committee headed by the Prime Minister and consisting of leading ministers, advised by a 'think-tank' of economists and scientists. The rationale was that unemployment was an overriding problem requiring the mobilisation and concentration of all the resources of government, as in wartime. Secondly, it distinguished between long-term planning for permanent economic reconstruction and short-term schemes for the immediate relief of unemployment. It argued that the long-term solution was a greater reliance on the home market, backed by a financial policy (directed by the state rather than banks) to provide credit for new industries and necessary measures of rationalisation. In the short term, the government should introduce limited public works, retirement pensions, the raising of the school-leaving age and an expansionist monetary policy. Overall, these proposals were fairly modest in comparison with later measures of Keynesian intervention and may not even have been sufficient for the task at hand. But they contrasted favourably with the barren approach of the government to economic problems.

The memorandum came to the cabinet on 3 February 1930, but Strachey had already leaked it to the *Manchester Guardian*. This meant that the cabinet, prompted by the aggrieved Thomas, spent more time discussing the propriety of Mosley's methods than the policies he was proposing. Discussions then dragged on until 20 May, when Mosley realised that he was isolated within the government, which was in receipt of totally negative Treasury advice on every suggestion he had made. He thus resigned (with Strachey), saying that the choice was between himself and Snowden and that the only 'clean thing' was to submit the issue to the test of party opinion.[3]

Strachey was as impatient as Mosley. In March he had already expressed some sympathy with the CP's view that the Liberal, Labour and Conservative Parties were essentially similar, although he maintained that the Labour Party still represented the working class.[4] He now actively supported Mosley's resolution to a PLP meeting which expressed dissatisfaction with the present unemployment policy of the government and called for the formulation of an alternative strategy. This view had considerable support in the party, but Mosley probably made a mistake in refusing to accept a compromise, for back-bench loyalty to the leadership was still very strong. However, Strachey encouraged him to insist on a vote, arguing that 'what the people want is action'.[5] The result was a total defeat for Mosley, who obtained the support of only twenty-nine compared with 210 for the government. However, the Mosley caucus now secured the adherence of two important recruits: W. J. Brown, who was the secretary of the PLP group of ILP MPs, and Aneurin Bevan, then a new young MP on the Left of the party. Despite its departure from the traditional left-wing approach of nationalisation and the establishment of a socialist economy, Bevan saw Mosley's programme as better defined and more practical than that of the ILP, and joined a group of sixty calling for Thomas's dismissal. He then collected a hundred signatures for a resolution to be moved at a further PLP meeting urging the government to adopt a bolder unemployment policy. However, he too found that government influence over MPs remained extremely strong, and the majority withdrew their signatures.

Strachey now campaigned energetically and enthusiastically for the Mosley Memorandum and may even have supported Mosley's efforts to secure support outside the Labour Party, particularly from younger radical Tories such as Boothby and Macmillan. Certainly Strachey was, by now, totally disillusioned with Parliament and accepted the need for a stronger executive, and this was part of the case that Mosley was putting to non-socialist 'modernisers' during the summer. However, Mosley was also now emphasising the theme of 'imperial unity' to insulate Britain and the Commonwealth from world economic pressures, and Strachey was less happy about this. He now shared the belief in the need for domestic protection, but was worried about the imperialist overtones in imperial unity. In fact, there had been underlying differences of emphasis between the two men and these were evident during the summer as Strachey tried to strengthen the left-wing orientation of the movement.

In the first place, he asserted that Mosley's Memorandum was justified only by the emergency and that 'sooner rather than later' the country's capital wealth must be publicly owned.[6] Secondly, he re-established his connections with the ILP, being one of only eighteen MPs who expressed their willingness to accept the policy of the extra-parliamentary organisation when voting in Parliament. Thirdly – and symbolically – he returned to the Soviet Union with a visiting party, which included Bevan.

At this time Strachey was not wholly uncritical in his attitude to the Stalinist USSR but he was already deeply attracted to it. In July 1928 he had described the atmosphere of the Soviet Union as 'astonishing and stimulating';[7] and he had devoted his maiden speech in the House of Commons to the need to increase Anglo-Soviet trade, informing Parliament that, in addition to the positive effects this would have in Britain: 'I do not feel ashamed to admit that I care very much about the benefits . . . which such a policy should bring to the workers and peasants of Russia. . .'[8]

The trip to the Soviet Union during the summer of 1930 reinforced his enthusiasm and the attempt to secure a pro-Soviet policy became a touchstone of his efforts to maintain a leftward influence on Mosley. On his return, he therefore drafted a pamphlet (published with Bevan and George Strauss), which again argued that the Soviet market was the one great opportunity remaining for Britain in the world. He was hoping simultaneously that Mosley would succeed in changing government policy on unemployment and that he himself could counteract the imperialist orientation of the alternative strategy with a pro-Soviet line.

By the autumn of 1930 it was clear that Mosley was going to make some kind of bid for leadership, and at the annual conference he made a rousing speech in defence of his memorandum. This appealed to the Left by urging the government to put a bold unemployment policy before Parliament and, if obstructed, to go to the country with a plan both for unemployment and for the reform of Parliament. Mosley received a standing ovation, almost secured a victory for the resolution, and was re-elected to the NEC. However, this may have reflected his charisma as a speaker and the rank and file's frustration at the government's sterile policy rather than any firm base in the party. By now there were signs of criticism within the ILP at Mosley's 'dangerous leaning towards a Labour Economic Imperialism',[9] and he was still actively trying to widen his appeal outside the party. Strachey was obviously aware of the differences between Mosley and himself, but hoped that he and Bevan would be able to maintain a more left-wing influence. However, when Mosley spoke in the House of Commons at the end of October, he did not mention public works, pensions or the raising of the school-leaving age, but placed all the emphasis on 'insulation' and the Empire. Strachey uttered his own *cri de coeur* in support: the government's measures, he argued, had no overall coherence and little relevance to the present situation, despite the fact that the world crisis would bring about greater unemployment and an attack on the wages of workers. Against this were Mosley's proposals:

> To many Members on this side that policy may have seemed novel, unorthodox and even fantastic. It certainly sacrifices – and everyone faces up to the fact that we must sacrifice – some of the economic doctrines we have held on these benches (and which I, for example, have held very strongly).

But:

> Surely in a situation so grave and menacing it is time for us to consider... proposals which may outrage some of our oldest and deepest prejudices but which yet obviously are, at any rate, on a scale, and systematic enough, to make some real progress to deal with this problem in its entirely?

He confessed that the policy of economic nationalism ran counter to internationalist principles but:

> We do not believe that we can get through the present crisis without national planning – that is certainly a well-established Socialist position – and we do not believe that it is possible that we can have national planning unless we have control of our own imports. We believe that this is an absolutely essential coping stone which must be placed on any edifice of our national planning.[10]

Events now moved fast. It was decided that the next step was to form a Mosley group in the PLP by inviting signatures for a definite statement of policy. Mosley's first draft was generally pushed to the left by Strachey, Bevan and Brown – the most striking aspect of this influence being the dropping of the imperialist theme. It was published on 13 December as an 'immediate plan to meet an emergency situation' and invited support from 'any in our party or the nation who agree... to state their agreement'.[11] The proposals were broadly similar to those in the

Mosley Memorandum, although executive dominance was now more pronounced. The statement called for:

(1) a cabinet of five ministers without portfolio, armed with 'power to carry through the emergency policy' subject only to 'general control' of Parliament;
(2) a national plan, with a basic premise that the home market is the basis of prosperity, coupled with an import control board, a commodity board, trade with all nations and Commonwealth agreements;
(3) a short-term policy of constructive works financed by loans, including, in particular, a massive slum clearance programme.

It ended with the same socialist gloss that Strachey had put in his speech to the Commons: 'We surrender nothing of our Socialist faith. . . [but] the immediate question is not a question of the ownership but of the survival of British industry.'[12]

The manifesto was signed by seventeen Labour MPs, nine of whom were ILP members, and also by A. J. Cook, the miners' leader with whom Strachey had collaborated so closely on the *Miner*. It was rejected not only by the PLP but also by the ILP. The reasons for this, and the effect of the rejections upon Strachey, merit further analysis.

The ILP, with considerable justification, tended to focus its attention on Mosley himself (as indeed did the Labour Party leadership). It therefore stressed the fundamental difference between itself and the Mosley group in relation to imperialism as against internationalism, and the search for a 'national' solution rather than a socialist one. In addition to these 'doctrinal points', there were extremely important institutional and organisational aspects to the dispute.

The formation of a Mosley group, without reference to the ILP, ran counter to the organisation's attempt to impose greater discipline on its MPs. Secondly, and still more fundamentally, the manifesto was calling for greater executive dominance and a limitation of parliamentary rights when the ILP was trying to reassert the right of its MPs to vote against the government. For all these reasons – and perhaps also the middle-class intellectual nature of many of the Mosley group – Maxton was delegated to ask all ILP signatories to remove their names from the manifesto.

Strachey was, no doubt, already disillusioned with the weakness and divisions within the ILP, and did not believe that it could act as a decisive force. Nevertheless, the break was of great significance. He had long since ceased to have any faith in the Labour government, believing that a microscope would be needed to 'find the least trace of Socialism' in any action taken by Snowden as Chancellor of the Exchequer.[13] He was also intolerant of the PLP, which had, in general, loyally supported the government. By severing his tie with the ILP, he was, in practice if not in intention, abandoning the Left. Apart from his general belief in the imperative need for an emergency programme, one further factor was paramount in this decision. He fully shared Mosley's exasperation with the House of Commons, for he was:

> tired of sitting quietly in the 'best club in the world' watching, from its comfortable armchairs, the slow decline of British industry and the rapid drift to disaster of the movement with which we are identified ... We cannot muddle through this time. That is the essence of our message...
>
> We recognise ... that the present parliamentary and governmental machine is incapable of carrying out such a programme as we have envisaged. A nineteenth century parliament designed for the sedate discussions of leisurely days and nights cannot conceivably look at the modern tasks. For parliament to insist upon the right to obstruct, to delay, to clog its own executive machine and yet not turn it out is to reduce Democracy to mere obstruction: ... and that has to go ... Maybe we have committed political suicide. Who knows, and who cares?[14]

Such attitudes could only drive him closer to the future leader of the BUF.

In January 1931 the Mosley group made one more attempt to secure a majority in the PLP, when Bevan proposed that the NEC should summon 'a special national conference to consider the unemployment crisis'. MacDonald tried to induce him to withdraw the resolution with the extraordinary argument that the crisis had passed its peak. When Bevan refused to do this, the combination of governmental pressure and back-bench loyalty again ensured a resounding defeat for the rebels by ninety-seven to thirteen at a PLP meeting on 31 January. Following this, the group set to work on a more comprehensive document on which their campaign could be centred. However, by now, Sir William Morris, the car manufacturer, had already handed Mosley a cheque for £50,000 to form a new party.[16] It is unclear whether Strachey and the other participants had any knowledge of this at the time, but by 20 February six members of the group had decided to resign from the Labour Party. At this point Bevan withdrew from the Mosley caucus, but Strachey was so convinced that the Labour Party was doomed to sterility that he was eager for the break. He insisted that it was the leadership which had betrayed socialist principles and, in his letter of resignation on 24 February, he told MacDonald that when he joined the party he had seen it as:

> a political instrument by which [a] new society might be realised; an instrument by which the workers might achieve their emancipation from a new totally unnecessary poverty and might realise their noble ideal of educational, social, and economic equality of opportunity.
>
> After nearly two years of this the second experience of a Labour Government in Office, I am convinced that neither the present Cabinet nor the Parliamentary Labour Party which supports it has the will to attempt any of these things.[17]

John Strachey

He would have preferred to form an independent socialist group but deferred to Mosley's wishes.

The New Party was thus launched by six labour MPs (one of whom, Oliver Baldwin, withdrew almost immediately); Allan Young, a close associate of Strachey and Mosley in the Birmingham ILP; and one Conservative, W. E. D. Allen. The main policy programme on which it was launched was entitled *A National Policy: An account of the Emergency Programme Advanced by Oswald Mosley, MP*. Despite this attribution of the programme to Mosley, Strachey chaired the drafting committee and worked on it with Allan Young, W. J. Brown and Bevan. (Bevan had not realised that the policy statement was to be the basis of a new party.)

The core of the economic argument of *A National Policy* was the proposal that Britain must control imports by the establishment of commodity boards. It also called for agreements with the Commonwealth and Empire which could, it claimed, insulate 40 per cent of British exports from foreign competition. Within this protected economy, the government should choose the forms of production best suited to the development of the home market at a higher standard of living. This would involve such measures as a national economic planning organisation, to plan the readjustment and rationalisation of industry; and a national investment board, to provide the necessary capital and to co-ordinate investment. It was also necessary to establish a stronger department of industrial and scientific research, to help promote industrial development and to implement a rational policy for the location of industry. State planning of the currency to prevent a fall in price levels (and the stabilisation of international prices by a cancellation of reparations and debts) was also seen as essential. In the short term, work could be provided on necessary public developments – above all, through state action to bring about slum clearance.

While this was all in line with Mosley's thinking, Strachey and his associates introduced a left-wing nuance into the economic programme. It argued that imperial agreements must not prevent the industrialisation of the non-self-governing Empire, for this would be a concealed form of exploitation. It added that trading arrangements could be made with other countries and, in particular, with the Soviet Union. And it advocated reductions in armament expenditure – a suggestion that never constituted a part of Mosley's argument.

No doubt Mosley accepted these points so as to maintain some left-wing legitimacy and because he was, in any case, comparatively uninterested in the details of the programme. For Strachey, they were no doubt important in enabling him to believe that the New Party was to be a movement of the Left. In fact, on its own, the economic programme was, in the context of the time, neither 'Left' nor 'Right', but unorthodox. It contained the kind of state intervention that could subsequently be implemented in a Fascist form. But it also foreshadowed many policies that would be introduced within parliamentary regimes after the Second World War. Its economic nationalism was also akin both to Fascist notions of autarchy, and to proposals such as the 'alternative economic strategy' favoured by the Left of the Labour Party in the 1970s. However, the programme as a whole appears more obviously anti-socialist if its overall rationale and constitutional proposals are considered.

While the manifesto countered the prevailing economic orthodoxy, it was equally insistent that socialism must be removed from the immediate political agenda for 'questions of the ultimate goal of society' were 'excluded by the very urgency of the problem'. As far as humanly possible 'employers and workers should meet the emergency by a common effort'.[18] In itself, this was little more than a call for 'consensus politics', although appeals to transcend divergent class interests in a situation of 'national emergency' are normally the tactics of the Right. This emphasis was reinforced by the programme's constitutional proposals.

The powers of Parliament were to be reduced, thus converting it from 'being a mere "obstructionist's paradise" ... into a true agent of the national interest', while the cabinet would be cut down to a small group of five or six ministers without portfolio, under the Prime Minister. This would enable effective action to be taken 'before it is too late' and reverse the situation in which the country: '... has never had a conscious policy for the last ten years, and has drifted hopelessly from one crisis to another.'[19] The closest parallel to this call for constitutional change is probably Gaullism rather than Fascism. Nevertheless, the seeds from which Fascism could grow are clearly evident in the programme as a whole. If the themes of class harmony, the suppression of ideological conflict, nationalism, leadership, action and anti-parliamentarianism became more pronounced, the New Party could be transformed into a Fascist movement. All this was implicit in the programme itself: given the nature of its leader and the political circumstances of the time, the transformation is scarcely surprising.

Strachey's association with the New Party lasted from its establishment at the end of February until 23 July, when he and Allan Young resigned, issuing a public statement that Mosley was moving towards extreme Conservatism or Fascism. During this five-month period, he put all his energies into the New Party's campaign and continued to propagate its line. He also sometimes used language and concepts which came nearer to Fascism than those in *A National Policy*. In June, for example, he wrote: '... we are a movement of revolt: we call on all that is sound, virile, and clear-sighted in the nation to rebel against the fatal acceptance of inevitable national decline'.[20] And in an article written with Professor Joad, he showed markedly corporatist tendencies in his constitutional proposals.[21] Yet Strachey was probably worried from the start about his decision to join the New Party.

His own retrospective account cited the party's first by-election, fought by Allan Young in Ashton-under-Lyne early in May, as the turning point. The local Labour Party was convinced that the intervention of the New Party, which obtained 4,500 votes, led to a Conservative victory, and a large hostile crowd assembled outside the Town Hall when the result was announced:

> It roared at [Mosley], and as he stood facing it, he said to me, 'That is the crowd that has prevented anyone doing anything in England since the war.' At that moment British Fascism was born. At that moment of passion, and of some personal danger, Mosley found himself almost symbolically aligned against the workers. He had realized in action that his programme could only be carried out after the crushing of the workers and their organizations.[22]

The experience of Ashton was equally important for Strachey, for the display of working-class opposition increased his unhappiness about his position. His desperate attempt to maintain a more left-wing line as Mosley moved towards Fascism brought about the final break in the summer. Three issues were to be of particular importance: the nature and use of the youth movement; the party's general orientation; and its international alignment.

After the Ashton by-election there seems to have been no disagreement, in principle, about the need to build a youth movement, and Strachey seems also to have accepted that young recruits needed to be trained to protect New Party meetings from disruption. According to his later account, the real dispute was over the *use* that would be made of the youth movement. That is, while Strachey wanted a force to fight on behalf of the workers, he feared that Mosley intended to use it against them. However, this claim needs to be treated with caution, because Strachey's political position had shifted considerably by the time he wrote this account, and he had come to believe that the working class might need to use violence to overthrow capitalism. In June 1931 he was still insisting, in public at least, that he fervently believed in a peaceful solution.[23] It is impossible to establish which of these two attitudes reflected his actual state of mind at the time – if indeed he even knew himself. Certainly for Joad – a close associate of Strachey's in the New Party – the whole idea of a youth movement with para-military associations was abhorrent. Strachey was, no doubt, divided between sharing Joad's revulsion and his own more Marxist conviction that the youth movement might be acceptable if it fought on the right side.

In any case, the conflict over the nature of the youth movement soon became involved in wider issues about the nature of the party and its internal organisation. For when, on 30 June, Strachey tried to counteract the Fascist overtones of a speech by Mosley, the latter publicly reprimanded him and made it clear that he would tolerate no independence within the movement. By now the disputes over the party's general orientation were also coming to a head.

Strachey accepted the need to attract backing from a wide range of social groups, but his main hope was still to secure working-class support for an expansionist economic programme. By the early summer, however, Mosley was seeking the sponsorship of right-wing financiers, politicians and newspaper proprietors. On 18 June, when Mosley prevaricated on his attitude to the exclusion of some categories from unemployment benefit, Strachey came to believe that there were strings attached to such support and that Mosley's economic policy was moving to the Right. Strachey's immediate reaction was to attempt to increase working-class and left-wing recruitment to the party, particularly by trying to induce A. J. Cook, the miners' leader, to join. But he had limited success and Mosley continued his discussions with Lloyd George and Churchill without informing him. Such divergencies over the party's general orientation were the fundamental reason for Strachey's defection, but the immediate cause concerned international policy.

As noted, the initial New Party programme had held the balance between Strachey and Mosley by maintaining the importance of expanding both intra-imperial and Anglo-Soviet trade. However, Strachey continued to press for a more active Soviet policy and Mosley eventually asked him to write a memorandum on the issue. Strachey now deliberately brought matters to a head by advocating not only a close economic partnership with the Soviet Union but also an intimate political relationship, and a weakening of the ties with France and the USA. In the Empire, policy should be confined to assisting 'the native races to build up economic systems suitable for them'.[24] Mosley predictably rejected the document, arguing that only a Communist could possibly support such a proposition. When it was put to the executive, Strachey and Young were outvoted by five to two and resigned.

Strachey had at last broken his ties with Mosley, and realised that he had made a terrible mistake in joining the New Party in the first place. But why had he done so? We have seen that Strachey believed that urgent action was needed to resolve the problem of unemployment, and that he thought that he and Mosley understood what needed to be done. His justifiable exasperation with the Labour leadership has also been demonstrated, as has his attempt to maintain a left-wing influence over Mosley, both before and after the creation of the New Party. Yet none of this accounts fully for Strachey's actions. After all, many others who remained within the Labour Party were equally frustrated with the leadership. In particular, it is fruitful to compare Strachey and Bevan in this respect, for they were very close to one another and, as already noted, Bevan had even joined Strachey in drafting *A National Policy*. But he had drawn back at the very last moment when it became clear that the New Party was to be launched outside the Labour Party. Why? What was the essential difference between the two?

There is some evidence that Bevan could see that the New Party would 'end up as a fascist party' and that it was for this reason that he rejected Strachey's attempts to persuade him to join.[25] But even if Bevan was not as prescient as this implies, there was a crucial difference between them, which Bevan himself tried to pinpoint when Strachey broke away from Mosley in July:

> It is the besetting sin of intellectuals to be too much influenced by the drive of their own minds. They are too reluctant to submit themselves to the pressure of events. In intellectuals, there is a tendency to want to dominate and shape these things arbitrarily. They can influence these events only by being moulded by them. Thus the profound difference between the typical intellectual and persons who, like myself, have the security of metaphysics on a social struggle upon which to rely in moments of doubt and uncertainty.[26]

Bevan was certainly right in believing that Strachey always wanted to control events. However, it is doubtful whether this was primarily because he was an intellectual. After all, many intellectuals are justifiably criticised for not wanting to *do* anything. What Bevan may really have meant is that the fundamental difference between them lay in their class backgrounds, a point which was put far more harshly by J. Johnson, the President of the Birmingham Labour Party from which Mosley and Strachey defected. Having described the experience of ordinary Labour Party and trade union members in working through organisations, and being forced to submit to majority decisions, Johnson continued:

> But the recent converts to the Party from outside the working classes have not had this experience. They come in full of enthusiasm, and in some cases, also full of ideas that will cure the world's ills

if only they are applied at once. They are impatient at having to submit their schemes and manifestoes [*sic.*] to the searching examination of men and women whose intellect they certainly think is much inferior to their own. That they should ultimately be turned down fills them with amazement and resentment. Not for them the more patient educational work required to convince a majority to their viewpoint. They will have their own way or get out. So they get out and proceed to form a Party all of their own.[27]

Of course, class background in itself is an insufficient explanation for Strachey's action. But if this is coupled with his particular upbringing and character, it does provide an insight into his decision to join Mosley.

Strachey might argue (as he had in 1929) that the labour movement must never cut itself off from the working-class, but Bevan's whole life was rooted in working-class politics. This meant that Bevan probably felt, almost instinctively, that it could not be right to step outside the Labour movement, even for a policy that made more sense than that which was likely to be implemented by a Labour government. In comparison, because of Strachey's combination of class background and character make-up, he could transfer his emotions on to a new organisation if the old one appeared stultifying. This also helps to explain a further paradox: his temporary suspension of Marxism.

Despite his theoretical belief that politics was the embodiment of class conflict, all his deepest instincts were to want to resolve the problems from the top with the minimum of fuss. Temperamentally, he still wanted to believe that there was a peaceful solution which could be implemented by rational, decent people getting together to sort things out. When the economic crisis developed, he thus recoiled emotionally from the idea of intransingent class conflict. He was desperate to find an answer to the problems and this expressed itself in impatience and contempt, not for the capitalist system, but for the Labour Party, Parliament

John Strachey

and tradition.

The final crucial factor – which also distinguished him from Bevan – lay in Strachey's attitude to leadership. One side of this was reflected in his wish to reform the machinery of government so that five pre-eminent people could institute authoritative decisions without real parliamentary control. No doubt such elitist assumptions – which perhaps included a belief that he himself would play a major role in the new institutions – stemmed from his upbringing. But the other side was his own deference to Mosley's leadership.

It is unlikely that Strachey would have taken any of the crucial steps towards the formation of the New Party without Mosley. Long after the break he was to describe himself in the years up to 1931 as one of 'Mosley's closest lieutenants',[28] and there is no doubt that this is the way he acted at the time. For, despite Strachey's powerful intellect and ability to inspire real affection, he lacked inner confidence and often deferred to those who seemed absolutely certain about the direction to take. In 1930-31 it was Mosley who seemed to embody the qualities which Strachey felt that he himself lacked. While constantly trying to maintain his own leftward influence, Strachey therefore generally deferred to Mosley's leadership and chose him in preference to the labour movement.

Because Strachey was so dependent upon Mosley, it took a great deal of courage to break from him. As he later confessed, about himself and Allan Young:

> we were willing to carry self-deception very far, much too far indeed, in order to avoid a break which was extremely painful to both of us. We pretended to ourselves that his talk about Fascism 'did not mean anything'.[29]

But there was a difference between 'self-deception' and support for Fascism. Strachey might have had some of the elitism, impatience for action and nationalism that were inherent in Fascism and he was temporarily prepared to see the solution to the crisis in terms of class harmony and corporatism. But even as a member of the New Party he vehemently condemned Nazism and, as soon as he became convinced that Mosley was intent on Fascism, he broke from him in full awareness that this would be deeply traumatic.

His personal life was also in a state of turmoil. His marriage to Esther was very problematic, and he was now deeply involved with Celia Simpson, whom he had first met at Oxford. She was the daughter of a vicar, and was a strong character with a deep socialist commitment. She shared his attraction to the Soviet Union and had accompanied him on the trip there in 1930. While Esther had worked with him in the New Party, Celia had no doubt encouraged him to make the break from Mosley. However, he had not yet taken any final decision to leave Esther and stay with Celia.

The summer of 1931 was therefore a very painful time for Strachey. Bevan recognised this but was overjoyed by Strachey's break with Mosley and looked forward to an immediate renewal of their political co-operation. At this stage Strachey himself probably had no idea what to do. However, the final collapse of the Labour government in late August clarified his mind, for he saw this as the 'last straw' for the Labour Party.

Bevan was therefore to be disappointed, for Strachey was now to shift direction once again. From the experience of his own traumas, and those of the Labour government, and reinforced by his increasingly close relationship with Celia, he would soon be inspired to produce the most powerful and influential books he would ever write. And he would write them in close association with the British Communist Party.

3 The thirties: Strachey's golden age

> I have a stock answer to dear old ladies who ask me 'and why Mr Strachey, did you become a Communist?' 'From chagrin, madam', I reply, 'from chagrin at not getting into the Eton Cricket XI.'

Between 1932 and 1939 Strachey worked in close co-operation with the British Communist Party. It was also the era in which he was most prolific as a writer, and he became a household name on the Left. His popularisations of Marxism were more widely read than those of any other British writer at any time, and vast numbers of people were converted to socialism during the 1930s, at least in part through his books. Nor was his influence confined to Britain. He was almost as well known in left-wing circles in the USA, where he wrote regularly and undertook a series of lecture tours. His books were published there as well as in Britain and were often addressed as much to American audiences as to British ones. Many future Third World leaders were also introduced to Marxism by reading the works of Strachey.

This chapter does not attempt a full summary of his activities or writings during these highly eventful and prolific years. It seeks instead to answer three questions: Why was Strachey a Communist? Why was he so remarkably successful as a writer and propagandist? And was there anything original or unusual in his Communism?

Strachey and Communism

From 1932 until the outbreak of war in 1939, Strachey effectively wrote and worked as a Communist. He described himself as a Communist, he consciously promoted the CP's line, his works were discussed with party leaders before publication and were influenced by their comments, and he tried to avoid writing anything which was inconsistent with CP policy. It is, nevertheless, worth noting that he was not actually a party member: when he applied to join in the summer of 1932, his application was rejected. At this stage, the leadership was happy to use Strachey's services by influencing his writing, offering him a position on the CP paper, the *Daily Worker*, and using him (with his consent) to try to induce ILP members to join the CP. The party believed that he could be useful as a fellow traveller but, in 1932, distrusted all intellectuals, particularly one with as chequered a career as Strachey. At the time, the rebuff was a major blow to him. Ultimately, his non-membership provided him with many advantages. He could honestly say that he had never been a party member – something that was to help him when facing a deportation order from the USA in 1935 – and as he became increasingly important as a Communist propagandist he had more direct access to party leaders and greater freedom than rank-and-file party members.

But why had he wanted to join the party and what was the nature of his Communist commitment? According to Strachey himself:

> The collapse of the second British Labour Government in the year 1931 was for me the decisive event. It was necessary for me to see with my own eyes and at close range the mingled impotence and treachery of social democracy in action ... in order to know that

this corpse would never rise again. Not until this indisputable evidence had been thrust upon me was I willing to admit that the British Social Democracy was not the friend, but the deadliest enemy, of the interests of the British workers.[1]

In fact, the second Labour government was a shattering experience for him in at least three respects. First, even during the first few months of the administration, when capitalism had still appeared stable, no significant progress had been made. At the time, Strachey had seen this as a failure of understanding and political will by the leading personnel in the Labour government, reinforced by defects in the machinery of government. By 1932 he had come to believe that the problem was far more fundamental and concerned the whole relationship between the state and capitalism, for 'the capitalist class owns and controls the governmental apparatus'.[2] Thus, even the initial phase of the MacDonald government may have undermined his faith in reformism. But it was compounded by the second factor: the world economic crisis. Whereas he had believed it essential for a Labour government to alleviate unemployment and poverty, it now seemed evident that the capitalist crisis was vastly exacerbating it. Finally, there was his own traumatic experience of attempting to find a 'third way', which had paved the way to Fascism rather than to the compromise solution he had been seeking.

All this probably brought Strachey close to despair. This feeling was mitigated by his relationship with Celia, but even this was not straightforward for he had not yet taken the final decision to leave Esther. These strains (perhaps reinforced by some worry about money) led to a nervous breakdown, followed by three years of psychoanalysis. However, Strachey was not a depressive or pessimistic person. He always wanted to believe that there was a rational solution to all problems, and that action was possible on this basis. And once he had decided what the solution was, he became *totally* committed to it. The fundamental impulse which drove him to Communism in 1931-32 was thus the belief that it was the way to salvation – the only way to maintain human civilisation once social democracy had failed.

Naturally, the fact that he had been influenced by Marxism since the late 1920s made it more likely that he would now turn to Communism. Yet this is less obvious than it appears. For in the 1920s he had regarded Marxism primarily as a theory which explained the underlying structure and motion of a capitalist economy. He now turned to Communism as an overall explanation of, and solution to, the problems of the world. In so doing, the real continuity was as much with the initial impulse towards socialism in 1924 as with the Marxism of the late 1920s. For, whereas he had originally seen reformist socialism as the only road to salvation, such hopes were now transferred to Communism. Strachey turned to Communism to maintain 'the eternal cause of human culture, of science and of civilization itself' in the belief that capitalism would become ever more barbaric.[3]

By late 1932 he was absolutely committed to the CP, which he was prepared to serve without being a member. By then he had taken the irrevocable decision to stay with Celia, who had been allowed to join the CP (perhaps because she had the impeccable qualification of having been dismissed from the *Spectator* for organising a pro-Soviet conference). They married in July 1933, after his divorce from Esther was finalised, and remained together until his death. This meant that his political commitment to Marxism could now be strengthened by his emotional life rather than being in contradiction with it, as in the late 1920s. Subsequent events reinforced his faith in Communism. The major event to have this effect was Hitler's accession to power in Germany in January 1933. For this meant that the 'barbarism' which he had seen as the inevitable result of capitalism in decline was given a more concrete form. From this time on, anti-Fascism became his overwhelming preoccupation in all his writings and political activity. In 1934, for example, he became chairman of the British section of the Communist-backed 'World Committee against War and Fascism' and its 'co-ordinating committee for anti-Fascist activities'. In this capacity, he played a leading role in organising opposition to Mosley's BUF, particularly in a vast rally in Hyde Park in September 1934, and participated in Communist-led international anti-Fascist meetings. For Strachey, the most urgent task of Communism was, henceforth, to save human civilisation from Fascism.

The second factor which strengthened his Communist commitment was intimately connected with anti-fascism: the gradual movement by the CP towards a united front and popular front line. Between 1928 and 1933, the Communist International's view of Fascism had been revolutionary in theory and complacent in practice. The argument was that Fascism was a reflection of the capitalist crisis which must ultimately lead to a Communist victory. Fascism could not prevent the collapse of capitalism and Communists did not, therefore, need to abandon their revolutionary purity in order to build an anti-Fascist alliance. The German Communists had maintained this line even while the Nazis had risen to power. In Britain, the results of the 'ultra-left' stance had been less catastrophic, but it had left the CP relatively weak and isolated. In 1929 its membership had fallen to under 3,000 and, although it doubled in the wake of the collapse of the Labour government, it was still comparatively powerless. Strachey had always been worried about the weakness of the CP. In December 1931, when he had first considered joining it, he had expressed the fear that it was too isolated from the workers to get 'any grip whatever on the mass movement' if the economic crisis developed quickly.[4] In November 1932 he again told Palme Dutt that he thought it imperative that the party should increase its size and cease to be 'exclusivist'.[5] And the major aim of his writing

The thirties: Strachey's golden age

was to broaden the appeal of Communism. Hitler's accession increased his anxiety to build a mass movement, and his enthusiasm for the CP grew as it gradually moved away from its sectarian line.

As far as Strachey was concerned, the change was far too slow and hesitant, and throughout 1933 and 1934 he urged the CP leadership to adopt the united front policy with more understanding of Labour Party susceptibilities. He warned that otherwise 'success is utterly impossible, and the only prospect in front of the British workers is massacre'.[6] He remained convinced that the building of an anti-Fascist alliance was the overwhelming priority, and the more fully the CP adopted this policy, the more harmonious was his relationship with the leadership. The turning point came in the summer of 1935 when the Communist International's 'line' changed very significantly. From then until 1939 the unity of the Left against Fascism became the overwhelming priority. The Communists were no longer particularly interested in demonstrating the inevitable collapse of capitalism: their most urgent desire was now to construct an anti-Fascist alliance with all 'democrats' at home, and with the Soviet Union abroad. In the later thirties the 'popular front' involved the dilution of a specifically socialist appeal, let alone a revolutionary one.

Strachey welcomed this attempt to create a mass movement against Fascism and, as he possessed consummate skills as a communicator of the Communist cause, he became increasingly important to the CP. The fact that he was not actually a member made him even more valuable to the party as a propagandist for the popular front. His opportunity to play a major role in this respect came in January 1936, with an invitation from Victor Gollancz.

Gollancz was not just a commercial publisher but a campaigner with an almost messianic sense of mission. He had quickly recognised Strachey's talent and had published three of his books by

1935. But in January 1936, passionately concerned about the threat of Fascism and war, Gollancz suggested that he, Strachey and Harold Laski should establish a Left Book Club. The objective of this was to promote a domestic popular front and a pro-Soviet alliance. Strachey and Gollancz ran the club in close collaboration with the CP and used the club to promote the CP line, without stating this publicly. (Laski was probably unaware of this connection; Gollancz became troubled by some CP activities by August 1938.)[7]

The purpose of the Left Book Club was absolutely in line with Strachey's wish to create a mass anti-Fascist movement on the basis of current Communist strategy. Indeed, it epitomised the nature of his Communist commitment and he devoted an enormous amount of energy to its activities. He and Gollancz selected its books (overwhelmingly pro-Communist and pro-popular front), and he spoke at numerous rallies and meetings. Above all he became its principal and most popular writer, with monthly articles in its newsletter, *Left News*, (initially *Left Book News*), the publication of two new books and a vastly successful pamphlet (and the re-publication of *The Coming Struggle for Power* on its behalf).

The Left Book Club was the most successful popular front movement in Britain, ultimately achieving a membership of 57,000, with 1,500 study groups. Its local meetings and major rallies were often far better attended than those of the Labour Party. Strachey was of immense importance to the club, as its dominant intellectual influence and he and Gollancz made a formidable team.

The Left Book Club and the popular front never dominated the British Left, for the Labour leadership remained adamantly opposed to any such movement. Nevertheless, it played an important role in popularising socialism and helped the CP increase its membership to 17,756 by 1939. Strachey, as its most

The thirties: Strachey's golden age

popular writer, played a very considerable role in influencing this movement of opinion.

If Strachey expressed his Communist commitment most enthusiastically when attempting to broaden its appeal and to create a popular front against Fascism, this did not mean that his adherence to it was superficial or diluted. During this phase in his life he was convinced that Marxism was absolutely scientific. As he put it:

> The claim is definitely made that the body of knowledge, and the method of social investigation, which we now possess, makes it possible to arrive at substantially certain, verifiable conclusions in sociology and political affairs. Thus the era of uncertainty, of guesswork, when one opinion was as good as another in such matters, since none could be verified, is over, and an epoch of genuine scientific investigation, in which facts and deductions can be tested and established, has opened.[8]

His closest friend, Robert Boothby, interpreted Strachey's attitude in different terms:

> the motive that has possessed you for the last ten years ... has been the urge towards Faith. Without it, you have felt life would be intolerable. So the struggle has gone on and on, now waxing, now waning, with many doubts and hesitations, moments of valour and moments of timidity, until one day – plop – you got it. And now there you are. Full of Faith! And happier than you've ever been.[9]

In fact, the two aspects of Strachey's character were – temporarily – fully integrated. He found the Communist version of Marxism totally convincing as an intellectual and theoretical system, and emotionally satisfying, particularly since Celia was at least as committed to it as he was. With this exhilarating sense of certainty, he could work for Communism in order to save civilisation from barbarism and Fascism.

Strachey as a writer

Strachey could not have made such an extraordinary impact unless the circumstances had been propitious. In particular, the conditions which persuaded him that the only alternatives were Communism or Fascism drove hundreds of thousands of others in Britain, continental Europe and the USA to the same conclusion. His message was, therefore, resonant at the time, and became more so as the international Communist movement embraced the popular front policy. The fact that the CP supported Strachey and promoted his work through the international Communist movement also obviously helped him. Nor should the role of Victor Gollancz be underestimated, for he publicised Strachey's writing, particularly after the formation of the Left Book Club. For example, when Strachey's *The Theory and Practice of Socialism* was published in November 1936, the club proceeded to set up a training school for group leaders who would go out to the groups and take study courses on the book over a period of four or five weeks. Lectures on it were given by all the club's top speakers (including Strachey himself) throughout the country, and study outlines were produced for it. Again, when Strachey's long pamphlet *Why You Should be a Socialist* achieved its amazing success in 1938, with over 250,000 copies sold in two months, it was the Left Book Club which promoted it and Gollancz who published it at 2*d* per copy.

Nevertheless, Strachey's own talents made all the difference. After all, he became so important to the CP *because* he demonstrated his ability to popularise its line even during its sectarian phase. His first book of the era, *The Coming Struggle for Power* was, in many respects, an 'ultra-left' work, but it still brought Communism to a far wider audience than it had ever reached before, and was perhaps the most influential book he

The thirties: Strachey's golden age

ever wrote. Similarly, while Strachey was helped by Gollancz and the Left Book Club, it was his writing which helped popularise the club. As the Left Book Club's national organiser later wrote of *The Theory and Practice of Socialism*:

> no single book more completely fulfilled the basic aim of the Club: to provide that disciplined study, rooted in fact and illuminated by theory, which was what the Club wanted to give its members. It stiffened the fibres of a Club whose sympathetic feeling and genuine passion needed precisely this basic *understanding* of the forces at work in capitalist civilisation.[10]

Nor could *Why You Should be a Socialist* have had such an impact without Strachey's unique ability to answer all the major questions of the time in an informed, persuasive and interesting manner within ninety-six pages.

The essential factor in Strachey's success was obviously his ability as a writer. An important aspect of this was his capacity to mount a compelling argument on a theme which addressed the most fundamental problems of the era. This was particularly evident in the book which he wrote while he was embracing Communism: *The Coming Struggle For Power*. The strength of this was not in its theoretical sophistication but in the way in which Strachey managed to convey one essential point across a vast range of subject matter. The writing style was beautifully clear, free from jargon and often humorous, but the 'message' was urgent and serious. For Strachey's purpose was to persuade the reader to share the conclusions that he himself had just reached: that capitalism would lead to barbarism; while Communism was the one hope for the world. He sought to demonstrate this not only historically, economically and politically but also in the spheres of rationality, science and culture.

Strachey's economic theory during his Communist phase will be considered in the next chapter. It is sufficient to note here that in *The Coming Struggle for Power*, he dismissed as irrelevant all the reformist ideas that he had previously embraced. Capitalism could not be planned because investment decisions were taken solely in accordance wth profitability. But, following Marxist theory, he argued that the declining rate of profit would lead to perpetual, and ever deeper, crises of stagnation and mass unemployment. The domestic repercussions would be increasingly repressive political systems, as capitalist interest sought to drive back gains that workers had previously won and to thwart the success of any new challenges. This would result in either overt Fascism or dictatorial systems based on existing state structures. In either case, the consequence would be violence against the workers. Overseas, a new impetus would be given to imperialist expansion as each capitalist economy tried to overcome its declining profitability at home by seeking new outlets abroad. The inevitable result of this would be another war between the imperialist states. There was no way, short of Communism, of preventing these horrific results which must inevitably follow from the decline and degeneration of capitalism. Social democracy was far worse than useless: it could not alter the course of capitalism but led the workers astray by claiming that it could. Social democratic parties thus: 'satisfy the workers' need to dream of socialism, whilst remaining tied to capitalism'.[11] The social democrat was 'a kind of inverted alchemist' who transmuted the gold of 'instinctive working class revolt... into the lead of working-class passivity and subservience'.[14] Social democrats, therefore, led the workers 'to ever new defeats, surrenders, deceptions and betrayals'.[13] Still worse, they acted as 'Social Fascists' by organising the workers for a form of capitalism which would, in its decline, become Fascist.[14]

Such arguments were within the normal range of 'politics', but Strachey enlarged the terms of the debate by demonstrating that 'civilisation' itself was becoming incompatible with the doomed system. Scientific progress should lead to the elimination of superstition and religion. However, because social progress had not matched scientific advances:

> a profound sense of disappointment and discouragement pervades the Western world ... In spite of the intellectual suicide involved, an increasing number of men turn away from science and reason, and seek again in desperation to believe in the consoling myths of the childhood of the race.[15]

Nor could science itself prosper any longer, for there was little point in explaining how 100,000 tons of steel could be produced if industrialists could no longer sell 1,000 tons. The decline of science would be gradual because it was still needed by war industries. It would take scientists some time to recognise this because: 'Most of them prefer to take up the much easier attitude that politics are all nonsense; that science is the only reality.'[16] Eventually, however, some of them would grasp the truth and 'prefer science to capitalism'.

Similarly, creative writing was thwarted for authors were led to contradictions and despair when they failed to understand that 'it has become impossible to comprehend or order the phenomena of our times without the use of dialectical materialism'.[17] For example:

> Lawrence, Proust and Huxley all exhibit ... the tragic view of life. They are inheritors of the great tradition of literature. They are undeceived as to the realities of man's situation in the universe. And yet ... the reader cannot help feeling that there is some other and far less estimable element in their pessimism; he detects something febrile, at its worst, something petty in their attitude to life. It is as if there was some element of confusion, of unconscious deceit indeed, at the picture of human life which they paint. This element arises from the fact that they all confuse the unavoidable tragedies of human existence in general, with the entirely evitable,

but at present growing and deepening tragedies of a specific system of society in a period of decay. They make no effort to show that the present horrible frustrations, deformations and agonies of men are due to the fact that they are for the most part still living under the degenerating capitalism of the twentieth century ... Since they do not extricate themselves from present-day society, since they are unable to stand outside of it, conceiving of a new basis for human life, they are themselves, inevitably, infested by their surroundings of decay.[18]

If capitalism was horrific in all respects, the alternative was Communism. The hope for the world, therefore, lay in the workers recapturing their organisations or forming new and reliable ones so as to institute the new system. In this way, scientists and writers would also find fulfilment for it would be possible to establish a viable and just economic system, to develop rationality and culture, and to prevent the drive to a new war.

Since 'Communism or barbarism' were the only two alternatives, the issue of violence was a 'red-herring':

The alternative to the violence entailed by the lifting of human life to a new level is the violence entailed by the decline of human society, the break-up of such world civilization as exists, the dawn of a new dark age of perpetual conflict ... Forward or back is ... [men's] only alternative. Nor will either road be smooth ...

The sufferings ... which the workers will have to undergo in order to establish and maintain their rule in Britain, will be incomparably smaller than those which face them as the inevitable consequence of deciding once again to fight their masters' battles for them ...

Instead of fighting, and that vainly, as they must if they remain under the leadership of their imperialists, to preserve all that is worst in the world, they will fight, if they fight for themselves, to secure a new epoch in the history of mankind.[19]

The Coming Struggle for Power obviously had some serious weaknesses. In particular, it showed a blind enthusiasm for the USSR. For example, the massacre of the peasantry undergoing forced collectivisation was simply described as the second critical period of the revolution: '... when the last substantial class of persons who derived their income from the possession of the means of production, the class of rich peasants, was dispossessed.'[20] And he claimed that in the Soviet Union, there was: '... an exhilaration of living which finds no parallel in the world. To travel from the capitalist world into Soviet territory is to pass from death to birth.'[21] Its explanation of almost all contemporary ills in terms of a declining capitalism was also sometimes simplistic. Yet even if these flaws are acknowledged, the book was a *tour de force*.

His argument that capitalism was doomed to collapse in Fascism and war had tremendous contemporary relevance. In November 1932, when the book was published, unemployment was still rising in the major industrial countries. Fascism and dictatorship were gaining in strength throughout much of the European continent, and the Japanese had carried out the first major expansionist war of the decade with the attack on Manchuria. Strachey's message that Communism was 'the one method by which human civilization can be maintained at all' was thus extremely persuasive. Moreover, every subsequent crisis of the 1930s appeared to reinforce his dire predictions: as the Nazis came to power in Germany, as the Italian Fascists attacked Abyssinia, as Franco launched a civil war against the Spanish republican government and as capitalism continued to stagnate, the essential argument of *The Coming Struggle* seemed to be confirmed in history. It was, therefore, a book for the whole decade, re-published in both Britain and the USA in 1934 and again in 1936 in the USA (when it sold 20,000 copies within months) and in Britain in 1937.

J. K. Galbraith was thus justified in later terming the book 'brilliant' and in saying that: 'As an exercise in persuasion, as distinct from the purely doctrinal rescripts issued by Lenin, Stalin and Mao, it was probably the most influential work of its kind in the century.'[22] And Richard Crossman later recalled its contemporary impact in evocative terms:

> to the Socialist generation of the 1930s, the Coming Struggle for Power came as a blinding illumination. Suddenly they saw the class war with Strachey's abstract extremism, jumped with him to the conclusion that capitalism was a doomed failure, and rushed to join the army of Socialist Revolution. So they dedicated themselves to the cause of the Spanish republic, of the hunger marches and of collective security against Fascist aggression ... This was a seminal book. Sown in the soil of the Hitler epoch, The Coming Struggle for Power produced a great tree of Socialist activity.[23]

One more example of Strachey's extraordinary ability to write a book for the times can be considered briefly.

In March 1933 the Labour Party rejected the CP's first proposal for a united front against Fascism and published a statement entitled *Democracy versus Dictatorship* as its response. Its argument was both straightforward and simplistic: 'dictatorship' and 'extremism' on one side always provoked their counterparts on the other:

> The follies and furies of Tzarism led straight to Communist Dictatorship in Russia ... The Communist dictatorship in Hungary was the pretext for the Dictatorship of Horthy. Italian Dictatorship tries to defend itself by saying that it saved Italy from Bolshevism ... The reaction of the upper classes throughout Europe has strengthened the demand for Dictatorship of the Working-class. The fear of the Dictatorship of the Working-class in turn has evoked the iron Dictatorship of Capitalism and Nationalism.[24]

The conclusion was that the rank and file must refuse to have any dealings with the Communist Party and confine their activities to peaceful, constitutional methods. This would prevent the upper classes from turning towards Fascism which was, in any case, regarded as a remote danger given the depth of democratic convictions in Britain.

Since Strachey was totally convinced that capitalism was in decline and that this would inevitably lead it to become increasingly repressive, the argument of *Democracy versus Dictatorship* appeared catastrophic. For if the labour movement committed itself to constitutionalism, while capitalism implemented an increasingly severe anti-working-class dictatorship, Labour's policy would inevitably deliver the workers to Fascism. He, therefore, wrote the *Menace of Fascism* with the deliberate intention of stimulating: '... the maximum amount of opposition to the "Democracy versus Dictatorship" line in the Trades Union and Labour Party'. He saw it as vital to bring about: '... *some REAL fight* against the English version of the policy of the lesser evil before it is too late'.[25] [original emphasis]. He sought to counter the Labour leadership's line by making 'an overwhelming emotional appeal, backed by solid reasoning'.[26]

The book was again immensely successful within the terms Strachey had set for it. It began with a powerful emotional appeal, quoting a collection of newspaper reports of Nazi atrocities against Jews and workers. Having given the reader this initial shock so as to counteract any complacency, Strachey explained, from a Communist perspective, the causes and nature of Fascism:

> as the movement for the preservation by violence, and at all costs, of the private ownership of the means of production. This and nothing else is the real purpose of Fascism. When we understand this, everything else in the madness of Fascism becomes comprehensible. Fascism will try to destroy in war our marvellous powers of production, and to crush democracy, pacifism, and internationalism because these things are becoming incompatible with capitalism. Fascism is the enemy of science, of rationalism, of educational progress for the same reason. Fascism kills, tortures and terrorises

> in defence of the right of capitalists to keep the fields, factories and mines of the world as their private property.[27]

This was followed by a detailed critique of the policies of both the German Social Democrats and the Labour Party in which he used his turn of phrase to its full advantage. Thus, for example, the belief that capitalists could be prevented from using violence if the Labour party reaffirmed its intention of establishing socialism peacefully was:

> like attempting to prevent the onset of a thunderstorm by affirming our belief in fine weather. Or ... like informing your opponent at a game of cards that, in face of his showing every sign of preparing to cheat, you promise, whatever he does, to abide by the rules.[28]

> ... in the long run the existence of democratic and liberal institutions ... are incompatible with the existence of Capitalism.[29]

> To suppose anything else is to suppose that the capitalists love democracy more than they love their property.[30]

Labour's policy was thus one of retreat, which would lead to a total loss of faith by the workers in their own institutions and their delivery to Fascism because of their despair and disillusionment. The only effective way to counter Fascism was by the opposite policy of active resistance: defending and enlarging every gain which the workers had won; pressing for higher wages, which would help to overthrow capitalism; and using 'every democratic right we have as weapons with which to develop the struggle of the workers'.[31]

The Menace of Fascism fulfilled some of Strachey's hopes. Obviously it did not bring about a united front, for this was an unattainable aim given the attitude of the Labour leadership. But the book became a text for the Left, including left-labour proponents of the united front. Strachey was able to promote the line of the book in debates throughout the country and in dis-

The thirties: Strachey's golden age

cussions with Labour party dissidents. He also played a key role in implementing the strategy as Chairman of the British section for the Communist-backed 'World Committee against War and Fascism'.

Nearly sixty years later, it is easy to criticise the book. We know that Fascism did not occur everywhere, and we can see that there were reasons why it was far less probable in Britain than Strachey believed. The National government provided ample power for the implementation of pro-capitalist policies, and the economy stabilised to a considerable extent by 1934. Nor was there the kind of 'total' crisis – national, cultural, economic and political – that had occurred in Germany or Italy. However, none of this was obvious at the time. Strachey could justifiably believe that the economic revival was both partial and temporary, and that the governemnt had no idea how to prevent a recurrence of uncontrolled slump. He also had good reason to share the widespread conviction that the National government – particularly in its police policy – was repressive in its attitude to the Left and unemployed workers and, at the very least, complacent in its dealings with the British Union of Fascists. His attacks on the supine attitude of the Labour leadership are also perfectly understandable. The assumptions of *Democracy versus Dictatorship* were simplistic and were used to justify a policy which was fairly complacent to the National government on the one side and bitterly anti-Communist on the other. In particular, Herbert Morrison's bans and proscriptions on an enormous number of united front and anti-Fascist organisations certainly weakened the Left and seemed designed to marginalise the most intransigent opponents of the National government and of Fascism.

Finally, Strachey had again written a book for the whole era, for much of subsequent history seemed to confirm the view that Fascism was inherent in capitalism. In February 1934 a form of clerical-Fascism massacred the workers of socialist Vienna and, in the same month, it seemed that French Fascists might attain power in France. Above all, the Spanish Civil War, which began in July 1936, appeared to epitomise the universal tendency for the extreme Right to declare war against the working class. When all this is considered in conjunction with the British government's appeasement of Nazism and Fascism, it was quite understandable that many on the Left believed or feared that the government would introduce Fascism at home or, still more probably, back a Nazi attack on the Soviet Union. *The Menace of Fascism* expressed all these fears and pointed out the alternative in a direct, accessible and plausible form.

The Coming Struggle for Power and *The Menace of Fascism* are just two examples of Strachey's prowess in arguing his case. Part of his strength was his sheer literary ability – something which actually led to the inclusion of his writing in collections of English literature. Whereas most Marxist writers are relatively difficult for the 'uninitiated', Strachey could persuade, entertain and explain simultaneously. Even the complex economic arguments in *The Nature of Capitalist Crisis* could be represented in such a way as to amuse the reader, thereby stimulating a greater effort to understand Marxist economic theory. Thus, for example, having presented a brilliant explanation and parody of marginal utility analysis, he concluded:

> The Catholic church only requires of its faithful a belief in the Virgin birth, the infallibility of the Pope (when speaking *ex cathedra*), in a few more dogmas, and in the usual miracles. These are light tasks of faith compared to those imposed on us by the marginal utility economists.[32]

However, Strachey was not just a brilliant writer: he changed people's perceptions by providing certainty in an era of uncertainty. As one obituary writer recalled, Strachey emerged as the one person who could explain what was happening in an age of bewilderment and fear:

> Strachey wrote those books in a strange, remote time. They were read by many young men on the edge of despair. And these men ... to whom John Strachey gave hope, remember him with gratitude.[33]

He did not only give them hope: he influenced them to join the Left Book Club and united front movement.

Although he was writing as a Communist with the intention of broadening the party's appeal, the Labour Party ultimately also derived a very considerable benefit from the club and his books. As he wrote much later:

> The Club was formed to prevent Hitler being allowed to start the Second World War, and to popularise Marxism in Britain. It succeeded in doing neither. But there was never a better case of failing to do what you intended, and yet succeeding in doing something quite different, but in the long run perhaps hardly less important. For what the Left Book Club actually did do was to play a considerable part in making possible the Labour victory in 1945.[34]

Despite its Stalinist excesses, Strachey's writing at this time favoured the Left as a whole, by helping to create a socialist climate of opinion. Many who later joined the Labour Party – even its right wing – were initially converted by Strachey's books. As Crossman wrote in 1956, *The Coming Struggle for Power* 'scattered its fruit over the back benches of the 1945 Parliament' and 'the bright young men of the present Shadow Cabinet prefer to forget that they were enthralled by ... [it]'.[35]

His success was not fortuitous. Convinced of the truth of Communist doctrine, and of the vital political importance of promulgating it, he regarded his writing skill as a talent which he could use on behalf of the movement. He wrote not only for his own satisfaction but in the conviction that he was serving a cause in which he fervently believed. For he felt sure 'that nothing successful' could be done until Marxism had been enriched 'with the great body of Anglo-Saxon culture' [36] and that he happened '... to be the only person who is putting over this particular information, which people desperately need today, in a form which they can comprehend'.[37] Such beliefs were the basis of his extraordinary power as a writer.

Yet his very success raises an important question. Was Strachey at this time an orthodox Communist who happened to possess extraordinary skills as a writer and propagandist? Or was he able to utilise these skills because he was not an orthodox Communist? In order to answer this it is necessary to reconsider the nature of Strachey's Communism.

Between two worlds

On the surface, Strachey appeared to follow the party line quite uncritically, while putting the message across in a superb way. For example, *The Theory and Practice of Socialism* was published in late 1936 as Stalin's purges, show trials, and executions were escalating. Yet Strachey eulogised the contemporary Soviet Union, which he saw as socialism in practice. Many non-Communist reviewers understandably found this abhorrent and contrasted the brilliance of the writing with the second-rate nature of some of the content. And, in general, Strachey suppressed his individuality in this period because he was convinced that the Communist version of Marxism was totally valid and he did not want to 'deviate'. (Indeed he had rewritten parts of *The Theory and Practice of Socialism* after Gollancz and the CP leadership had criticised it for being too 'lukewarm' about Communism.) However, there were some signs of originality in his thinking, particularly in his attempt to synthesise Marxism and Freudian psychology.

Strachey had long been interested in psychology and its

relationship with politics. In the 1920s he had tried to explain middle-class adherence to socialism in psychological terms, and had argued that psychological insights needed to be integrated into socialist theory. This long-standing interest had been reinforced by his own breakdown and subsequent analysis. These experiences heightened his general belief in the need for Marxists to recognise the importance of psychology both in their theories and political practice. More particularly, it confirmed his view that political attitudes were the result both of objective circumstances (as argued by Marxists) and of subjective, psychological ones. About himself, he thus said:

> Many and deep, I am sure are the personal neuroses which have made me into a communist. All sorts of conflicts made it necessary for me to rebel against society. But does this fact about my character prove that communism is a neurotic illusion? I do not think so. Neurotic illusions may have decided that I, John, rather than you, Tom, Dick or Harry should have become a communist. But the existence of the worldwide movement of the revolt of the working class is real, is objectively determined, and has nothing to do with the personal flaws and faults of any of those members of the intelligentsia who support it.[38]

A fairly typical Communist view was that it was not important to discuss individual motivation: it was sufficient to appreciate that the working class as a whole would adopt socialism because of the objective development of capitalism. Strachey disagreed. As far as he was concerned, the scientific nature of Marxism as a general explanation of the development of capitalism and the inevitability of socialism was an established fact. Yet it was equally important to understand both individual and group motivations, for the pace of change, and the ability of Communists to influence opinion, was crucially dependent upon this understanding.

His most theoretical elucidation of his viewpoint was given

in his preface to a book by R. Osborne, entitled *Freud and Marx*, which he sponsored for the Left Book Club in 1937. In this he advanced the argument that Freudian theory might be a 'dialectical opposite' to Marxist theory, thereby providing far greater insight into the Marxist notion of 'false consciousness'. Marx's great discovery had been that 'man's consciousness is determined by his social existence', but this needed to be understood in precise detail. The Marxist prediction that the consciousness of the need for socialism would develop automatically with the development of the objective circumstances had not been fulfilled. It was, therefore, vital to understand the way in which consciousness developed from social existence, and this was obviously more complex than Marx had believed. The principal conclusion of psychoanalytic theory is:

> that the emergence of a particular type of consciousness ... must not be conceived of as the passive reflection of a given social environment. It must be conceived of rather as the interaction of the social environment with certain dynamic, subjective urges within the man himself.[39]

This, he claimed, was quite consistent with the outlook of Marx and Engels, but Marxists tended to concentrate almost exclusively on the objective, structural nature of capitalist society. In the last century, this had been justified, but:

> Today, however, an increased emphasis should, surely, be laid on the subjective, dynamic factors innate in men, which the objective, environmental factors interpenetrate, to make man as we know him? For the environmental factors are all upon our side already: they cry aloud for social change. Our business is to see to it that we know how to interpret that inarticulate cry in such a way that men will heed it.[40]

Elsewhere Strachey used such psychological insights not only to explain why socialism had not come about but also as one part of the explanation for the prevalence of false or dangerous beliefs, such as Fascism.

Although *The Menace of Fascism* was, in the main, an exposition of the CP's interpretation of the phenomenon, Strachey was unlikely to be satisfied with this explanation. For it was a 'reductionist' approach in which Fascism was seen *solely* as a result of 'capitalism-in-crisis'. Other factors – historical, psychological, cultural and political – were either ignored or played down as 'bourgeois' explanations. But Strachey had to come to terms with the fact that he himself had 'been the dupe of the very attractive façade of Fascism'.[41] This was partly why he was so preoccupied with it and hated it so intensely. But because he was always interested in psychology, it also meant that he would want to explain the attraction of Fascism in wider terms than those used by conventional Communists.

In *The Menace of Fascism* he had explained his own involvement in psychological and political terms, whilst still putting forward the Communist interpretation as the fundamental explanation for Fascism as a macro-phenomenon. It was, therefore, not surprising that he sought the same kind of multidimensional explanation for ordinary workers, and in *The Theory and Practice of Socialism* he discussed this explicitly. Workers, he claimed, do not like being told by Marxists that class conflict is the fundamental feature of the capitalist system and that they must inevitably become involved in violence until the economic organisation of society is transformed. They would prefer to believe that their troubles are slight and easily remediable. Fascists played on this by telling them what they wanted to hear – that the class struggle would disappear if the agitators were removed. Moreover, Fascists also tried to banish class conflict from consciousness and, therefore, devoted a major effort to diverting workers' antagonism to capitalists onto other nationalities.

Once in power, Fascists had led whole nations down the path

of fantasy and wish-fulfilment:

> Experience derived from individual psychology should enable us to understand how a whole people may be successfully induced to take the word for the deed, to accept a subjective change in their own psychologies in lieu of an objective change in the environment; to make believe, to pretend, as a child does, that a passionately desired change has taken place. Such deceptions as this, the Fascists have shown, can be perpetrated upon a whole nation. But they can ony be perpetrated at the price of an ever growing divergence between the ideas in the minds of the members of such a nation and their real environment. Such a divergence between concept and reality, when pushed beyond a certain point, is called madness. And it is an undeniable fact that the Fascist propagandists are able to produce collective delusions in the population subjected to them, delusions which have pathological aspects.[42]

Strachey's psychology may not have been particualrly profound, but this attempt to marry Freudian insights with Marxism provided a far richer explanation of Nazism that the purely reductionist interpretation normally offered by the Communist movement. It emphasised the irrational aspects of the phenomenon as well as providing a fundamentally Marxist analysis of its economic basis. It may not have been as sophisticated as the work of Wilhelm Reich, who was developing a more famous theory of the mass psychology of Fascism (of which Strachey was probably unaware), but it was more immediately plausible and anticipated post-Second World War attempts to combine Marxist and psychological insights into the nature of Fascism.

However, the CP did not like this whole approach. As far as conventional Communist analysis was concerned, the Leninist party itself should guarantee the development of Marxist awareness amongst the working class. Analysis of either individual or mass consciousness in psychologiccal terms, therefore, constituted a bourgeois deviation, and Strachey was criticised for his approval of Osborne's book.

Although he did not develop his psychological analysis of Fascism any further, he did relate psychology to the area in which he was himself supreme: political communication. For he was convinced that Marxists needed to find the correct, psychological approach which would enable their audiences to grasp and act upon their message:

> Acquaintance with psycho-analytic teaching can help us to exhibit a cetain temper of the mind, a certain attitude to our fellow-men without which a political cause ... can hardly make its way.[43]

In other words, he was certain that the manner in which something was said was crucial: unless the message was expressed properly it could never have the desired effect.

However, this brings us back to the question of whether Strachey's emphasis in language and tone was a matter of tactics or whether it suggested a more fundamental difference between himself and the Communist Party. He argued (and perhaps thought) that the issue was primarily about style rather than political doctrine, and he constantly criticised the leadership for conducting its propaganda in a counter-productive way. Yet he also believed that manner, style and tone of voice:

> reveal the basic attitude of a writer or speaker to what he is discussing. That is why the workers are perfectly justified in attaching a high importance to this question. It will not be until all the spokesmen of scientific Socialism have satisfactorily adjusted their own attitude to the Labour movement that they will succeed in carrying the workers with them.[44]

And in 1938 he argued that the failure to create the widest possible popular front was, to an appallingly large degree, 'our fault':

> Only too often we have stated our case in the worst possible way.

John Strachey

> Only too often we have been strident, abusive, dogmatic, supercilious – all the things which the shrewd, practical workers of the movement hate, and rightly hate, most.[45]

Strachey may have really believed that he was talking just about political style, but something far deeper was involved. In reality, the Communist movement – following Lenin – used words as political 'sledge-hammers' to attack class enemies and to define the right line for its followers. Strachey may have been justified in believing that this was counter-productive. But he felt it so strongly because he was still alienated by it himself. Even when most fervent in his support for Communism, he had one foot in the non-Communist world. This, indeed, was why he was so effective as 'the revolutionary ambassador that Marxism sent to the middle class to argue the proletarian case'.[46] It was because one part of him continued to think in non-Communist categories. He could, therefore, put the Communist case in the most persuasive terms possible for non-Communist progressives and socialists.

This does not mean that he was insincere in his Communist commitment during his 'golden age'. On the contrary, he was, as has already been noted, fervent in his support for the movement. Once he had adapted to the psychological changes involved, he was also probably happier than at any other stage in his life. He had an exhilarating sense of fulfilment in carrying out work which he believed to be vitally important; his relationship with Celia was personally and politically close, he had two young children, plenty of friends and enjoyed the comradeship of the party. Communism also provided the certainty and authority both of doctrine and leadership for which he seemed to crave.

Yet he remained 'bourgeois' in a sense noted by a Soviet writer who, in 1935, commented on *The Coming Struggle for Power* as follows:

> He openly tackled the question, not from the standpoint of the working class, but from the standpoint of the interests of human civilisation. One clearly feels that had there been any possibility of preserving the bourgeois system healthy and progressive, Strachey would not have been for changing it, but inasmuch as he sees the impossibility of so preserving it and the impossibility of it being progressive, he courageously and irrevocably takes his stand with the class which alone can save civilisation, even though this be at the price of jettisoning its bourgeois content.[47]

This judgement was extremely perceptive and Strachey himself implied that this was the basis of his position. More than once he explained that he had not wanted to become a Communist:

> the whole folly (and worse) of the New Party adventure, was, for me, at bottom, one last desperate and reckless attempt to avoid becoming a Communist. For the practical and personal consequences of support of the communist cause was [sic] so serious; the readjustment of long-ingrained hatred is so difficult to accomplish; the adaptation of the bourgeois to the imperative need of the working-class movement for discipline, and the relegation of personal consideration to a sphere of very secondary importance, are to many people so painful, that every bourgeois intellectual will always try to avoid becoming a communist if he possibly can. More and more we shall all find, however, that the price we must pay for remaining in the capitalist camp is our complete intellectual and moral prostitution.[48]

The basis of the commitment was, therefore, the belief that Communism was the sole way of saving civilisation. He openly stated that if capitalism could be reformed so that it did not lead to barbarism, communism would not be necessary.

During the Communist phase his belief was, therefore, total but vulnerable. Mirsky was wrong in seeing it as 'irrevocable', for it could be undermined by either of two eventualities: a renewed conviction that capitalism was reformable; or a realisation that Stalinist Communism was not, after all, the saviour of the world. Between 1938 and 1940 Strachey was gradually led to both beliefs and was to suffer a new crisis and change of direction.

4 The break and the reconstruction (1940–45)

In April 1940 Strachey broke with the Communist Party by writing a letter to the *New Statesman* repudiating its policies. He knew how much he would suffer from this action, telling Dutt, his CP mentor:

> I realise to the full how utterly politically homeless this makes me: and, how easily complete personal and political degeneration occurs in such circumstances. Everything that you all will necessarily think and say of me will be hard indeed to bear. But I am what I am, and only worse deception and disaster could come from my pretending, to a still further degree, to be something which I am not.[1]

The subsequent months were at least as difficult as he had anticipated and he was later to describe the break as 'the most severe experience of his life'.[2]

The separation was still more traumatic than his break from Mosley, partly because it was the second time that he had had to renounce long-term political stance, and partly because his theoretical and emotional commitment had been so total. As Hugh Thomas noted, the trauma was to have long-term effects:

> when he abandoned communism, a spark went out of him which was never really rekindled. For he had placed all his creative power and physical energy at the service of something which he had believed to be a general guide to rational politics. But now Reason had failed him.[3]

He gradually recovered his faith in rational politics and, by 1942, had once again transferred his allegiance to the Labour Party – an allegiance which he maintained until the end of his life.

The object of this chapter is to explain Strachey's break with Communism and his reconstruction as a Labour Party politician.

Patriotism

One crucial factor in Strachey's break from Communism was his deep-seated patriotism. After 1932 this had normally been submerged in rhetoric about 'proletarian internationalism' and anti-imperialism. Even then it had surfaced occasionally in forms which he himself saw as deeply contradictory. For example, in October 1933 he wrote to the editor of the *Spectator* deploring its association with another journal, *Everyman*, which he regarded as Fascist:

> I suppose it is illogical of me. For I regard as inevitable that Capitalism as it declines will throw over board all decency, all humanity, all culture, all respect for truth and honour. But when I see this process going on, when I see the decline from the Spectator to Everyman I cannot help being affected. For although I am a Communist I cannot, inevitably disassociate myself from my background and my upbringing. I cannot help remembering that my family has contributed something to the culture of British Capitalism. And 'though in my view that culture is now entirely decadent, it was undoubtedly in its time one of the highest in the world. So I cannot pretend that I do not resent the Spectator – with which my family was so closely associated – being connected with such a publication as Everyman.[4]

In general, such sentiments were compatible with the popular front strategy of seeking the widest possible unity against Fascism. However, as the threat of war increased, Strachey's patriotism became more dominant. In the immediate aftermath of the Munich crisis in the Autumn of 1938, he told Robert Boothby:

> The issue during the coming months, and years, if we have so long, is that of the independence of this country. It is not a question now of whether this country is to become socialist or remain capitalist – or any issue intermediate between these two. It is a question of whether or not we are to be free to choose what we are to become. If a mixture of liking for the German and Italian Regimes, and terror of war, is to govern our rulers' world policy, we shall very soon cease to be a free and independent sovereign state in the full meaning of the word. Hence the issue must be presented to the British people in that form. The Freedom and Independence of Britain from a foreign tyrant; the oldest and deepest theme in British public life. Patriotism in its very highest sense.[5]

He emphasised that it must be a 'popular patriotism' to save democracy and conquer unemployment, and this was still in harmony with CP policy in 1938. However, Strachey's language and tone indicated that his strategy was based in fundamental beliefs and emotions rather than political expediency. Such sentiments partly explain why the signing of the pact between Nazi Germany and the Soviet Union in August 1939 came as a shattering blow to him, and he now told Boothby:

> You can imagine how staggered I am by the Soviet–German pact. My friends on the left say that it is not inconsistent with an Anglo–Soviet pact of mutual assistance...
>
> As you can imagine, I must pin all my hope to this view, for if it were to prove ill-founded, and the Soviet Union were to go into benevolent neutrality to Germany, my whole political position would be shattered. I should have to reconsider everything.[6]

He was reassured by the CP's initial stance on the war. This was to maintain the anti-Fascist commitment by declaring, on 2 September, a war on two fronts – against both Nazi Germany and the Chamberlain government in Britain. However, on 24 September the British representative at Comintern headquarters arrived from Moscow and informed the Central Committee that the war was, after all, an 'imperialist one' to which Communists must give no support. Palme Dutt now took the lead in pushing through this line and 3 October it was accepted by twenty-one votes to three (with Pollitt in the minority). The party issued a new manifesto on 7 October which declared that:

> It is not a war for the liberties of small nations. It is not a war for the defence of peace against aggression . . . The British and French ruling class are seeking to use the anti-Fascist sentiments of the people for their own imperialist aims.[7]

Four days later Dutt replaced Pollitt as General Secretary.

Once the immediate shock was over, Strachey's reaction was to justify the party's new line as if he had no doubts about it. In private, however, he tried, with increasing desperation, to convince the new leadership that 'war on two fronts' was the only acceptable stance. The Soviet Union's attack on Finland in November exacerbated his worries, which were now becoming known, at least amongst other CP fellow travellers.

Finally, he could stand it no more and it is significant that patriotic sentiments were to the fore in his letter to the *New Statesman*. Following the German attack on Norway and Denmark, the *Daily Worker*, he argued, had expressed the view that Britain and France had 'the exclusive guilt'. The paper now seemed 'not anti-war but pro-German' and he was convinced that the CP leaders:

> are prepared, for the sake of what they consider to be the interest of the Soviet Union, to give way to Hitler to any extent, and that they are utterly irresponsible as to the consequences to the British people of such unlimited giving way. So long as that remains the case I, and, it seems, almost everybody else in the country, can have nothing to do with them, however much we; like all sane people, 'do not want the war', and however much we may agree with them

as to the general character of the war.[8]

Once he became convinced that the CP leadership would tolerate a Nazi invasion of Britain as a means of saving the Soviet Union, he felt that he had no choice but to break away from Communism.

The importance of patriotism as a crucial factor in his break with Communism was also demonstrated by his subsequent development. In the summer of 1940 he volunteered as an Air Raid Protection warden. He reacted to the courage shown by ordinary Londoners during the Battle of Britain in a moving, but deeply sentimental, way, sending the following 'invocation' to Hitler:

Pay attention, Hitler. You have scattered the nations; you have easily deceived the statesmen, the generals, the bankers, the diplomatists, Marshals of France, Kings of the Low Countries, Czech democrats and Polish dictators, British Prime Ministers, Dutch Queens, Norwegian parliaments and Soviet Commissars; these and many more you have exactly known. Each you have broken or bought, or agreed with.

Now, however, you have to deal with a different kind of people. You have encountered the unemphatic and the unassuming ... They have had the temerity to survive your bombs. Moreover ... they have become not less, but more, themselves. They have become less, not more, like you: they have become less, not more, neurotic, unbalanced, fierce, cruel, and suspicious.

Pay attention, Hitler. You have the insight of genius. You cannot pretend that you do not know that it is either you or them. You must break them or be broken by them. Therefore send your bombers ... Spare no means ... All is at stake.

But ... Make haste or their quietness will echo round the world; their amusement will dissolve Empires; their ordinariness will become a flag; their kindness a rock, and their courage an avalanche. Make haste. Blot them out, if you can.[9]

At the beginning of 1941 his patriotism was given a still more concrete form when he was accepted into the RAF. His eminently upper-class background superseded the recruitment officers' concern about Strachey's Communism (although this delayed his initial promotion into responsible work). Once he was fully accepted, his talents and energy again led to a speedy elevation. He became enthusiastic about the camaraderie of active military service and was soon to act as a public relations officer for the war effort. Indeed, by 1945 he had become pre-eminent in this field, with highly acclaimed radio broadcasts justifying British military policy.

But if patriotism was a crucial factor in his break with Communism, it was always coupled with other values of equal importance. Above all, it was inseparable from Strachey's fervent anti-Fascism.

Anti-Fascism

It is hardly surprising that anti-Fascism continued to play a major role in his political development. As noted in Chapter 3, it had become his most fundamental preoccupation. Communism had been seen as the sole way of defeating Fascism and saving civilisation. The Nazi–Soviet Pact had, therefore, been shattering, not only for patriotic reasons but, still more fundamentally, because the homeland of Communism had been prepared to compromise with the most bestial form of Fascism. However, Strachey had been prepared to accept this action as a legitimate use of *realpolitik* by the threatened Soviet state. What he could not stomach was the CP's policy once he came to believe that it was prepared to accept the possible Nazification of Britain as a means of relieving the pressure on the Soviet Union.

When he broke with Communism he thus constantly reiterated his belief that the CP's single most important mistake was that it was '... grossly under-estimating the strength and importance of Fascism; it is slurring over to a fatal extent the difference between Fascism and the older forms of Capitalism'.[10] He believed this so deeply that it shook his faith in the scientific certainty of Marxism. He explained this in theoretical terms in an essay on 'totalitarianism', *The Betrayal of the Left* (1941), and made it the theme of a novel which he wrote at the same time. The leitmotif of *The Frontiers* (eventually published in 1952) was, thus, the importance of fighting against Fascism even if victory was unlikely. He now argued that actions which 'feel right' should not be disregarded:

> For it may be that what we do from our hearts – which means what we do in accordance with the standards which have been bred up in us – it may be that it is just these actions, and these alone, which will prove to have been justified. For, however hopeless and purposeless they may seem to us ... it may be that these actions alone will stand well.[11]

Once Strachey saw victory over Nazism as essential in both patriotic and anti-Fascist grounds, he was prepared to accept all means to this end. He therefore became a propagandist for Bomber Command, justifying the saturation bombing of German civilians in the last stages of the war. On this occasion, the general tendency to give total commitment to the causes he embraced meant commitment to 'total' war.

His patriotism and anti-Fascism were so profound that it was inevitable that he would break with Communism once he believed that it was betraying these values. But his action was reinforced by a further crucial factor: the belief that there was, after all, an alternative means of defeating Fascism. It is worth examining Strachey's search for an alternative, and its role in his political development, in some detail.

The alternative

Strachey's Communism had been predicated on the assumption that the capitalist system was doomed and must lead to continual slump and political repression. In *The Nature of Capitalist Crisis* (1935) he had given a brilliant explanation of the underlying Marxist economic theory on which this prediction was based, arguing that the declining rate of profit accounted for all the symptoms of degeneration and crisis. His conclusion had been that the more quickly people understood the truth of Marxist theory, the less blood and agony would be involved in the inevitable transition to socialism. At this stage he had rejected all proposals for economic recovery within capitalism as '... reckless and convulsive efforts, which, while they bring relief, bring it for ever shorter periods and at an ever higher price'. Reformist palliatives were not only economically ineffective but also politically dangerous, for they could reconcile the working class to a system which was bound to become increasingly repressive.

However, almost immediately after the publication of *The Nature of Capitalist Crisis*, the CP had adopted the popular front line. Since this involved the attempt to build an anti-Fascist front with non-Communists, there was less emphasis on the ultimate collapse of capitalism. Strachey himself followed this by proclaiming the need for immediate political unity and suggesting to non-Marxists that:

> If it turns out that the progressive programme ... can be carried through, peace can be saved, democracy preserved, and the standard of living raised without transferring any means of production ... you will simply have the laugh of [*sic.*] us.[13]

It is unlikely that he was ever satisfied by this stance. As a political economist, he was bound to be interested by developments in non-Marxist economic theory and practice, and the popular front brought Communists into discussions with young Labour economists through various organisations. All this inevitably stimulated Strachey's interest in the issue of whether there were any possible lines of development within capitalism other than the dire prognostications he had outlined in *The Nature of Capitalist Crisis*.

It was not just an intellectual interest. By April 1938 Strachey was already desperately worried that Communism in its current form might not, after all, defeat Fascism. His anxieties were recorded in a remarkable letter to his analyst in April 1938, three months after he had consulted him for the first time for some years. Apart from reiterating his criticisms of the CP for underestimating psychology, Strachey's main concern was that Communism would fail or even prove counter-productive. He saw the future in terms of an unending series of world wars between rival empires of a Fascist type and feared that:

> if I and my friends go on on present lines, we shall just about raise enough opposition to make it necessary for the British governing class to resort to repressive measures of the characteristic fascist type, without there being any real prospect of shaking their position.

He believed that the prospect of war and Fascism was objectively produced by the failure of the capitalist economic system. But he feared that this also produced conditions in which 'hate impulses are bound to arise in the masses of the population' and:

> if this is so, it is futile and actually pernicious for us of the Left to attempt to get the workers to repress those hate impulses. If we do so we shall merely alienate the workers from us and force them to express their objectively caused hate impulses through the destructive, irrational Fascist channel.[14]

In other words Strachey was losing his confidence in the ability of the CP to convince the working classes that their grievances were caused by the capitalist system. He now feared that there was no prospect of undermining support for Fascism unless economic maldistribution 'was put right'. This meant that it was vital for the Left to tackle the fundamental economic problems. Simultaneously, there was a need for a new political strategy which could counter Fascism without either precipitating it or being 'colourless' and, therefore, unappealing.

These beliefs soon crystallised into a conviction that it was essential to devise an economic counterpart to the popular front programme. He told his CP mentor, Palme Dutt:

> if, for good or evil, we have adopted People's Front Politics, we must have a People's Front economics also. If we do not, the result will be not that we avoid being involved in a Reformist economic policy, but that we get involved in a thoroughly bad Reformist economic policy.[15]

And he became deeply involved in the attempt to formulate an alternative strategy. He thought that such work was compatible with Communism – indeed that it was crucial for its future. However, it was a personal search for a solution to the problems and he was aware that Dutt might 'object strongly to some of my line'.[16]

By the summer of 1938 he was sufficiently impressed by some developments in reformist economics to state:

> the efforts of Mr Roosevelt, though many of them, to my mind, have been misdirected, and the recent theoretical work of Mr Keynes, have shown us that powerful weapons are at the disposal of a resolute progressive government which is confronted with a slump.[17]

He was now working hard on the book which would contain his alternative policy and was submitting drafts to Communist and non-Communist economists for criticism. By the time the war began, he had become convinced that he had formulated a viable strategy. Indeed, he probably repressed his doubts about the CP's general line on the war because he was so busy finalising the book, which was to be published in January 1940 as *A Programme for Progress*. He was also devoting all his energies to the attempt to persuade the party to adopt this strategy with the slogan 'Banks for the People'. (This was a shortened version of his ideas, also published in pamphlet form.)

A Programme for Progress encapsulated Strachey's theoretical and strategic thinking on political economy at the time. Although he subsequently broke away from the CP, for which it had orignally been conceived as a strategy, he remained committed to the broad outline of his programme until the end of the war. (Indeed he retained many of the ideas until his death.)

A Programme for Progress was a highly innovative work. One of its central features was to absorb the insights of Keynes's *General Theory of Employment, Interest and Money* (1936) into a socialist strategy. Keynes had shown how the state could intervene in the capitalist economy to create full employment and expansion. This had provided a theoretical rationale for the abandonment of the budget-balancing orthodoxy which had undermined the second Labour government and contributed to stagnation and mass unemployment throughout the inter-war period. The implementation of policies based upon Keynesian theory would transform industrial capitalism after the war (until the 1970s when the phenomenon of 'stagflation' and the reassertion of right-wing economic orthodoxy curtailed its influence). In a sense, then, the extent to which Keynes's thinking was understood was a test of the sophistication of other reformist economic proposals of the era. Viewed in this way, *A Programme for Progress* was unusually advanced, for Strachey explained and applied Keynesian insights in an original way. As Crossman wrote, in 1956:

> The impact of a revolutionary idea in politics is always slow. As far as I know, only one book was written in the 1930s which attempted to explain the General Theory to the rank-and-file Socialist and to evolve on the basis of it a practical policy for a Left-wing Government. That book was *A Programme for Progress* . . . Far in advance of its times . . . it still provides an excellent theoretical account of the problems which faced the Labour Government and the methods by which it overcame them . . .
>
> In the 1930s the history of western industrialised society changed course; and John Strachey, after a false start, grasped the significance of the change and successfully predicted the new direction. He took three years to accept Keynes, whereas most of his colleagues took twenty.[18]

This conclusion is reinforced by Elizabeth Durbin's important book, *New Jerusalems* (1985), which shows that, despite major innovations by young Labour Party economists after 1931, Keynes was still viewed with some suspicion. Contemporary evidence provides further confirmation that Strachey's insight in recognising Keynes's importance was greater than that of Labour's professional economists. Douglas Jay, who was a firm advocate of redistributory taxation, told Strachey that Keynes's multiplier was 'a red herring' and that he had led people onto the wrong track with his emphasis on investment. This involved too great a stress on public works and the rate of interest, leading eventually to armaments expenditure.[19] Similarly, Evan Durbin told Strachey that Keynes's conception of the marginal propensity to consume was a logical tautology, which therefore said nothing about the real world or the real relations between consumption and investment. Because of this he could not accept Keynes's explanations.[20]

But Strachey did not simply adopt Keynes's theory. He was highly critical both of his general attitude to capitalism and of specific parts of his proposals. For example, he condemned

Keynes for viewing propensities to consume and save as psychological characteristics of the population. Strachey argued that, for the masses, spending was a matter of capacity rather than propensity. He also endorsed the socialist emphasis on redistribution, which was not stressed by Keynes, and he maintained that socialists must use public works for socially useful ends rather than simply as a means of stimulating economic activity. He did not abandon socialism in favour of Keynes. He tried to provide a synthesis based on theoretical insights from Marx, Keynes and younger Labour Party economists, and the practical experience of the New Deal and other innovations in contemporary capitalism.

There was also an important sense in which Strachey had a wider understanding than Keynes himself. Keynes could see a way of overcoming economic stagnation, but he perceived it in terms of economics largely divorced from politics. For Strachey the issue was not simply technical or theoretical in this sense. He saw that the question of whether or not a progressive economic policy would be implemented was dependent upon the class and political forces which predominated at the time. He was certain that a new form of capitalism would emerge, but also saw that the system could favour the interests of either progressive or reactionary forces. He was, therefore, proposing a programme around which the Left could rally support and on which a progressive governmental strategy could be based. Keynes's approach was far more limited than this.

Strachey explained his fundamental economic assumption, and its difference from conventional Communist thinking, as follows:

> the main economic conclusion at which we have arrived is . . . that we cannot hope to combat stagnation unless we can increase the share in the final product going to the mass of the population. This is an exceedingly familiar conclusion: it has been common ground

> to much liberal and socialist opinion for many years. But such opinion has, naturally enough, been unwilling to give weight to the conservative objection ... 'But if you do that, you will destroy the motive of production. You may make production possible by supplying a market. But, nevertheless, production will not take place, for it will have become insufficiently profitable.'
>
> Many Marxist economists have given full weight to this objection (as I attempted to do in *The Nature of Capitalist Crisis*). They described this dilemma, and indeed emphasised it. They pointed out that the dilemma was, in principle, insoluble, and then left it at that. The capitalist system had come to an *impasse*; it must be, and would be, abolished. I have come to believe that such a conclusion is irrefutable, but, in a sense, abstract, and therefore misleading in practice. It is all-important to see that this is the basic nature of the economic problem which confronts us. But that does not mean that nothing can be done about it. The dilemma of profits or plenty cannot be solved so long as the decisive part of production is carried on for profit.
>
> That is why socialism is the only final solution. But there are ways and means by which the consequences of the dilemma can be for a time and to an important extent, combated, though only by means of modifying the nature of capitalism to [a] serious extent.[21]

The way in which he tackled the problem of the falling rate of profit will be considered later, but it is first worth noting that he had also shifted very considerably on the specifics of reform. In *The Nature of Capitalist Crisis*, he had relied both on Marxist economic theory and Hayek's monetarism (as outlined in *Prices and Production*, 1931) to demonstrate that increases in the money supply 'must sooner or later result in a boom and then a crash'. This was so because it distorted demand in favour of consumption, thereby increasing the price of production goods and removing the incentive to produce. Strachey had not, of course, accepted Hayek's solution of a permanently fixed supply of money, since this would depress wage levels to the lowest possible level and increase inequality. But at this stage he was convinced that the New Deal was doing exactly the same thing in a different form. For Hayek and Roosevelt were using alternative expedients to restore the rate of profit. They:

> are . . . two different ways of cutting down the effective purchasing power of individual consumers (predominantly wage-earners, of course). The inflationary method does this by raising (or preventing the fall of) the price-level and so making people's unchanged money incomes buy less than they would have done. The Hayekian wage cutting method does the same thing by the more simple and direct route of taking some of their money away.[22]

In fact, Hayek's method would have much to recommend it in comparison with monetary expansion since it led 'to less confusion and instability' and meant that 'the wage earner is openly instead of secretly robbed'.[23]

However, in *A Programme for Progress*, he explained that '. . . I have come to believe that expansionist measures, if they do form part of . . . a general progressive programme can be an indispensable step in the right direction'.[24] While reaffirming a Marxist definition of money as the 'objective, unconscious, incarnation of the social nature of wealth',[25] he now thought that: '. . . by the time that the disproportions caused by the creation of new money begin to develop, it will be possible to check, and ultimately cure them by means of social controls specially designed for that purpose'.[26] Such considerations convinced him that in economies like Britain and the USA, 'attempts to meet the chronic economic stagnation of our times by methods which involve the creation of new money' provided the best means to 'advance towards that complete social control of production which is the sole final remedy for our troubles'.[27] Monetary expansion was, thus, a vital element in his strategy.

He still highlighted the declining rate of profit as the fundamental tendency within capitalism. It was this which caused the more visible problems of mass unemployment and economic stagnation. He also continued to reject the expedient of simply increasing wages so as to cure under-consumption because this would further reduce the rate of profit. Indeed, he believed that a progressive government might even need to restore the rate of profit in some circumstances. However, he insisted that this could be reconciled with an increase in the real incomes of the mass of the population. The solution lay:

> in increasing the share of the mass of population in the national product at the expense, not of the profits, but of the other two subdivisions in the share of the product going to the owners of the means of production – namely, rent and interest.[28]

A Programme for Progress then sought to explain how these goals could be achieved. The first element in the six-point programme would be an increased use of public enterprise which, following Keynes, Strachey believed could have a multiplier effect on the economy. A combination of public and private enterprise, which had already been attempted in slum clearance schemes, could be vastly extended. Secondly, the rate of interest should be reduced so as to stimulate investment. This would help public utilities and local authorities, in particular, and would have some effect in reducing the costs of production without diminishing the purchasing power of the masses. Thirdly, since the working classes spent a higher percentage of their incomes than did the wealthy, redistribution would stimulate the economy and provide more work in consumer industries. However, such redistribution needed to be achieved without directly decreasing the rate of profit. The solution here was a greater progressive element in taxation policy (though Strachey did not believe that this could go too far without causing a prohibitive fall in 'confidence' and a decline in investment). Fourthly, direct distributions of money should be given to the mass of the population, particularly through increased old age pensions and children's allowances. This should be 'new money', until the point of full employment was reached, at which stage the payments should be financed out of taxaton so as to prevent inflation. This led to the fifth point, which was a prerequisite for monetary expansion: the establishment of a publicly owned and controlled banking system. At present the banks operated in the interests of capital and not those of the economy as a whole. They, therefore, had no incentive to adopt expansionist policies, either by lowering interest rates or by increasing the money supply, for profits came from rationing credit. The success of the programme, therefore, depended on the conversion of the banking system into a national service. Finally, it was also vital to control the export of capital and all purchases of foreign money, assets and securities by British citizens. All the available evidence, he argued, showed that the export of capital was the favourite method by which the owners of property undermined a progressive government (he cited the example of the French popular front).

His rationale for his programme was important in that he believed it added a crucial dimension to familiar, redistributory proposals. It was:

> designed to increase, almost at all costs, and whatever obstacles stand in the way, the total of the national income. The main emphasis has been laid upon these latter measures. For these are the measures which are designed to combat unemployment and stagnation in all its forms. These measures are designed to keep the very maximum possible proportion of the available means of production working at full pressure, and so overcome that chronic idleness of men and machines which has become the most horrible of all the curses of our society. Such measures are the decisive ones. On their success or failure everything depends.[29]

In other words, Strachey was putting full employment as the primary economic aim, just as he had done before his Communist years. It is also notable that he had rediscovered the importance of monetary expansion and the nationalisation of the banking sector – ideas which had been central to the *Revolution by Reason* in 1925.

The central political assumption of *A Programme for Progress* was that progressive forces might assume control of the state in a situation 'in which they cannot attempt the total and immediate abolition of capitalism and the capitalist state'. In these circumstances: '. . . they must, on pain of irreparable discredit, attempt to develop what may perhaps be described as a transitional, modified, controlled economy'.[30] This was so, not only because this would benefit the working class economically, but also because failures, like those of the second Labour government, were politically disastrous.

If workers:

> associate slump, unemployment, insecurity and all its attendant horrors, with the progressive side in politics, then they will turn to almost any form of reaction, even if that reaction lowers outrageously their share in the national income.[31]

This could mean both an increase in support for the extreme Right and the consolidation of Fascist systems in power. For Strachey saw that the Nazis had learnt to control the economy while liberal governments had failed to do so. There were, therefore, only two possibilities: either the system would be controlled by progressive forces which managed 'both to keep the wheels of production turning to the full and simultaneously to raise the consumer power of the population';[32] *or* it would be controlled by Fascists, in the interests of monopoly capitalism, leading to war production and aggression.

He accepted that there was no guarantee of success and that

the programme would be bitterly opposed by many capitalist interests. On the other hand, it was possible that intermediate sections of the population and some sectors of productive capital might rally to the progressive forces on the basis of such a programme:

> In a word, the programme cannot possibly avoid the struggle, but it can join issue on ground upon which the popular, democratic, progressive forces are at their strongest and reaction is at its weakest.[33]

The Communist Party and *A Programme for Progress*

Strachey attached enormous importance to this book. He thought it contained a strategy which was economically and politically feasible, and which offered the sole means of defeating Fascism and bringing the Left to power. He told his American publisher in March 1940 that it 'represents the only things I am really certain about, and therefore really care about in the world at the moment'.[34] He had regarded it as crucial that the party should adopt it.

In fact the CP hierarchy was never entirely happy with this aspect of Strachey's work and had criticised its early drafts. However, the whole thrust of CP policy between 1935 and 1939 had been anti-Fascist alliance and, in this context, proposals for practical measures to be taken by a popular front government were acceptable. In particular, Maurice Dobb, the CP's principal economic theoretician, was generally very positive about the later drafts of Strachey's work. (The leadership was probably always doubtful about the whole notion of amelioration within capitalism.)

Once the party adopted the new policy of total denunciation of imperialist war and British monopoly capitalism, such practical proposals were seen as irrelevant or even dangerous. Since the leadership was now attacking anyone who supported the war (i.e. those in the Liberal and Labour Parties whom it had previously been wooing for an anti-Fascist alliance), any suggestion that a popular front government might make an impact upon monopoly capitalism was regarded as diversionary.

A Programme for Progress had been completed in November 1939 – before the new line on the war had been implemented in its entirety – and Emile Burns, a leading member of the Central Committee, had offered some faint praise for the final manuscript:

> There are still many points on which I don't feel your argument is sound, but you have guarded against my main original criticism – that it glossed over the question of political power, and was far too optimistic about the 'full employment' possiblities. Therefore I think the book in its present form can't be taken as simply creating illusions, and some of the positive points are useful.[35]

However, during the winter the party's attitude to the war hardened still further, and in February Burns reviewed the book in the *Daily Worker* in a totally hostile way. Under the heading 'Strachey Progresses Backwards' he claimed that it was:

> in itself an expression of social democracy or reformism, the adaptation of working-class policy to capitalism. It is in effect to stand aside from the actual struggle against the war; to assume the defeat of the working-class in the struggle against capitalism and to ask what policy a defeated working-class is to carry out if, in spite of its defeat, it somehow crawls into 'power' but not 'full power' and is unable to abolish capitalism.

The review paid no serious attention to Strachey's economic arguments but was basically a 'hatchet job' which concluded:

> The important point is that the whole theme of Strachey's book is not Marxist, but Social Democratic; that it does not help forward the working-class struggle, but . . . divert[s] the workers from the actual struggle.[36]

The break and the reconstruction

The leadership's attitude to Strachey's cherished strategy, coupled with its whole appraisal of the war, was devastating for him. As he told Dutt, it reinforced his decision to break with Communism:

> Not, I hope, by way of personal pique, but because I see that the whole conception of an interlocking economic and political struggle, which ... I have always held, and which ... seemed not to be in conflict with the party's view during the People's Front, is now regarded simply as a 'reformism'.[37]

Communism no longer appeared to be saving 'civilisation' from Fascism and it had rejected the alternative programme which could, he believed, do so. It was clear that his crusade for the Communist cause was over.

Political reconstruction

A few months before his break with Communism, Strachey had distinguished between his position and that of Keynes:

> Keynesism, as Keynes as understands it, that is to say as a method of carrying on capitalism indefinitely, or at any rate for a generation, is completely fallacious ... I would say that ... an expansionist programme must break down or lead to full socialism – not in a generation, but in ten years at the very utmost, and more likely in two or three years, but that even so expansionism is absolutely vital to us precisely as a technique ... beginning the revolution ...
>
> I believe expansionism is only of value if it is conceived strictly as a weapon of a powerful people's government, a weapon being used ruthlessly against monopoly capitalism, but a weapon which has the supreme advantage of making it possible to keep the wheels of production turning at full speed while this phase of the struggle is being waged.[38]

In the months that followed he continued to claim that he was a Marxist (even a Marxist–Leninist) and that it was he, rather than the CP, who was applying Marxism–Leninism the more faithfully. He acquitted himself quite well in the mutual polemics with the party, but the controversy was ultimately sterile. Both sides could provide theoretical rationalisations for their positions, but Marxist theory was not the *primary* consideration for either of them. The CP leadership had adopted its line because of Comintern orders in the interests of the Soviet state, and Strachey had formulated his strategy because he had come to believe that capitalism was reformable, at least in the short term.

In reality he was searching for a 'non-catastrophic way forward' which would prevent 'the struggle developing into civil war'.[39] As soon as he came to believe that some advance was possible within capitalism, he had resumed his pre-Communist wish to find a peaceful way of resolving class conflict.

Once he broke with Communism, there was no going back. He was not impressed by the fact that the party reverted to a popular front line after the Nazi attack on the Soviet Union in June 1941. By now he saw Soviet Communism as a system which had adopted the principle that no price was too high to pay for its self-preservation. This had led, at the least, to 'the putrefaction of some elements at the centre of the system'. Enormous achievements remained: 'But the creative side of the revolution is spent. A great cause has turned into a great nation.' Of still greater relevance was the decline of international Communism where:

> An arbitrary bureaucracy has made a desert and called it party unity. An unscrupulousness for unscrupulousness' sake has become the established method of political activity ... Here too a profound inhumanity has appeared.[40]

Later in 1942 he argued that the goal of international revolution was no longer possible. The vision had gone 'bankrupt' because of profound party errors. When European revolution had not come about in the 1920s the Communist International should have been liquidated and the split in the international labour movement ended. Party members should have rejoined their indigenous labour movements (however reactionary) where they could have been invaluable. Instead, CPs had become more and more isolated and sectarian, except during the popular front period. Meanwhile the Soviet Union, in surviving, had changed and ceased to be the fatherland of the Western working class. Instead 'Marxist thought and feeling became incredibly rigid, dull, dead.'[42]

Strachey felt sure that he could see the faults of Communism and the pattern of post-war development. Sometime in 1942 he wrote to Celia, who had been in Canada with the children since July 1940 (so that Strachey could escape more easily in the event of a Nazi invasion). He explained his view that:

> Over the past ten years, both in practice and in theory (Keynes; New Deal; The Nazis; Sweden) *capitalism has learnt how production may be carried on, even though the profit motive is failing*. [original emphasis]

This meant that there would never again be a slump on the 1929-32 pattern for:

> Every genuinely independent State will set up a more or less controlled economy which will work more or less well, will be more or less reactionary (on the Fascist model) or more or less progressive (on the New Deal model). *This is what will happen*: whether we like it or not. And *nothing* could be so hopelessly un-Marxist as not to see that once this has become possible it has become inevitable. (And I am still a Marxist). [original emphasis]

He was convinced that controlled economies would emerge and that life could either be 'very decent or utterly intolerable' depending on the result of the war. The first necessity was to defeat the Nazis and then to ensure the maximum approximation of the new controlled economies to Socialism, with the minimum

Fascist element in them. This involved the 'steady shifting of the balance of class forces from the monopoly capitalists to the people'.[43]

His only remaining dilemma was to decide how these goals could best be achieved, for he was torn betwen a liberal view of individuality and morality, on the one hand, and his Communist past, on the other. It was not yet clear which would predominate and early in 1942 he attempted a new synthesis.

This took the form of a proposal to a few close associates, including Victor Gollancz, Allan Young and Sir Stafford Cripps, to establish a new association. He attached particular importance to the organisational principles on which his projected body should be based. Leninist parties, he argued, had failed disastrously in the West because they had tried to impose a particular type of doctrine. But such associations – emulated in antithetical form by Fascist parties – had shown both a strong psychological appeal and an outstanding organisational ability. He therefore argued that it was vital to establish an organisation of this type (though not a party) to act as a 'prime mover' both at the centre and throughout the periphery of a modern economy. It would be concerned with high-level theorising, partly because this was a means of ensuring true and unforced like-mindedness among its members. More fundamentally, the development of political and economic theory would create a body of people with superior insight into the trend of current events. All must, therefore, equip themselves with a sound knowledge of Marxism and Leninism, and other recent developments in capitalist economic practice and theory, as well as in psychology. There was also a need for work on the theory of the state, based on the writings of Engels and Lenin, but developing '... historical and contemporary research on the question of the extent to which the state apparatus can, mainly by balancing class forces, become an independent force itself'.[44] The decisions of the organisation's conferences must be binding on all members, for centralism was the key to the dynamic power of all bodies of the new type. Individualism must, therefore, be suppressed: 'For acceptance of a common bond of this degree of tightness is the key to effectivenesss in the contemporary world.'[45]

The proposal came to nothing for Gollancz and Young, in particular, were extremely critical of Strachey's apparent wish to create a new secret society, based on a distrust of the intelligence of the masses. But it is notable that, despite his break from Communism, he was still toying with the idea of a vanguard organisation, armed with a thorough understanding of Marxist theory, as the vehicle for the promotion of social and political change. He was still divided between conflicting emotions and theories. However, he was soon to resolve his inner conflicts.

The rejection of his proposal was his last initiative of this type. He had been in the political wilderness for two years and, when his somewhat eccentric notion of a quasi-Leninist association proved abortive, he turned back to the Labour Party. (His projected association had not been incompatible with Labour Party membership in any case as it had not been seen as a political party.)

Strachey's re-entry into the Labour Party proved as easy as his original adherence. Harold Laski was the mediator, suggesting Strachey as a parliamentary candidate in Dundee and facilitating Strachey's acceptance by party headquarters. Early in 1943 he was officially adopted by the constituency. In this position, he looked forward to the end of the war and the election of a Labour govenment to push a controlled economy towards socialism. Having adopted this theoretical and practical stance, he told Celia (who probably remained much closer to the CP) that this was the future prospect as he saw it: '... and I must admit I feel cheerful about it: *always provided we can beat the Nazis*'.[46] [original emphasis]

Despite the New Party episode and almost nine years as a

John Strachey

Communist, there was much continuity in outlook between the politician who had left the Labour Party in 1931 and the one who rejoined it in 1942. In both cases, Strachey was inspired by a personal version of Marxism but wanted to see change come through parliamentary means. In both cases, he was convinced that capitalism was an unstable system, with a tendencey to produce mass unemployment, but that it could be reformed by determined politicians using modern economic techniques. In both cases, he believed that monetary expansion and control over the banking system would be crucially important policy instruments. As he was also to achieve high office in the post-war Labour government, a casual observer could be forgiven for believing that the intervening years had been unimportant as far as Strachey's career was concerned. But this would be a superficial judgement. Certainly, there were great continuities between the Strachey of 1929 and the Strachey of 1945. But then there were also continuities with the intervening years, when he had believed that the salvation of 'civilisation' depended upon emergency measures or Communist revolution. Moreover, his subsequent career would be marked by these intervening years. He could never forget – nor would he be allowed to forget – that he had spent his most creative years outside the framework of mainstream politics.

5 A government minister (1945–1951)

> I have never had ... [an] inbred 'sense of the House'. A lot of my speeches ... have been open to that deadly, if affectionate barb ... 'Too deep for his hearers and always refining / He thought of convincing while they thought of dining.'

On 26 July 1945 Strachey was returned as an MP for Dundee and, for the first time, a Labour government was elected with an overall majority (of 146). To Strachey's great surprise, the new Prime Minister, Clement Attlee, offered him the post of Under Secretary of State for Air. He did so in the belief that Strachey's Communism was now a thing of the past, and that his years in the RAF had 'taught him about men and matters he might not otherwise have met' and that he now 'had his feet on the ground'.[1] Strachey was to remain a minister throughout the life of both Attlee governments: at the end of May 1946 he was promoted to the position of Minister of Food, where he remained until the General Election of February 1950; and from then until Labour lost a second General Election in October 1951, he was Secretary of State for War.

Despite the pressures of office he continued to theorise about politics. In 1949 he amazed Arnold Toynbee by sending him detailed comments on his multi-volume work, *A Study of History*, comparing and contrasting it with Marxism. And in 1950 and 1951 he delivered a series of speeches and lectures which attempted to consider the progress of the Labour government and the future of British socialism. Many of his conclusions foreshadowed those which he was to explain more fully in his books after 1951. There was also a considerable degree of continuity with *A Programme for Progress*, which he felt that the govenment was, to a great extent, implementing in practice. Indeed Strachey's ability to think theoretically about policy in a long-term context, while acting as a minister, was extraordinary. However, in these years he was, of necessity, primarily a political actor rather than a theoretician, and the main focus of this chapter will, therefore, be upon his ministerial role.

The first government (July 1945–February 1950)

Whereas the minority Labour governments of 1924 and 1929–31 can justifiably be regarded as failures, any judgement of Attlee's first administration must be more complex. For it was during these years that Labour constructed the post-war settlement. At home, it introduced welfare capitalism based on infrastructural nationalisations, full employment and a free National Health Service. Abroad, it played a crucial role in establishing the NATO alliance, which consolidated American influence and the divisions of Europe. These may be regarded as major achievements or lost opportunities, but Kenneth O. Morgan's judgement is probably a fair one, at least with regard to the domestic record:

> it is easy to go too far in criticizing or debunking the Attlee government. Arguments from hindsight often neglect the realities actually confronting the administration ... Critiques of that government in particular tend to underestimate the overwhelming financial and economic pressures resulting from the loss of overseas assets, the imbalance of trade, the loss of markets, the shortage of raw materials, and the vast dollar deficit which was the government's *damnosa hereditas* from the war years and from the pre-war heritage of industrial decay. In large areas of policy, the Attlee government had a clear record of achievement and of competence, which acted as a platform for successive governments, Conservative and Labour,

throughout the next quarter of a century.[2]

Strachey certainly had no qualms about active participation in the first administration, and was convinced that it was modifying the capitalist system in a progressive direction.

In general, he was regarded as one of the left-wing ministers in the government, and was probably the most consistent supporter of Bevan, the Minister of Health, who was the standard-bearer of the Labour Left. Early in 1947 they thus attempted to persuade Ernest Bevin, the Foreign Secretary, to follow a more pro-Jewish policy in Palestine (then a demand of the Left) and, later in the same year (and again in 1949), they both pressed for the continuation of the steel nationalisation policy when some ministers urged a slow-down because of the major economic crises then confronting the government. However, the view of Strachey as 'left-wing' needs to be balanced by the following factors.

First, there were few fundamental ideological conflicts within the government during this period, despite these occasional skirmishes. There were certainy latent divisions but, during Attlee's first administration, they were held in check largely as a result of the influence of Sir Stafford Cripps. He was Chancellor of Exchequer from November 1947 and gained the respect of both the 'Left' and 'Right' within the government.

Secondly, by mid-1947 the government as a whole accepted Bevin's interpretation of world affairs as a conflict between Soviet Communism and Western democracy, even when this had major repercussions on the domestic situation. For example, by 1948 the leadership sought to purge the Labour Party, the trade union movement and the Civil Service of Communists and fellow travellers, arguing that Communist parties were following Soviet instructions to sabotage Western economies. This was endorsed by Bevan and Strachey, both of whom served on the Cabinet Emergency Committee, which, in July 1949, recommended the use of emergency powers and troops to break a dock strike. The committee minutes imply that the real grounds for this action were not to prevent perishable food from going bad (as was maintained in public) but to defeat the 'Communist poison'.[3] Neither Strachey nor Bevan was at the forefront of such action, and Strachey probably disagreed about any early use of troops but he 'was strongly in favour of bringing in the Emergency Powers'.[4]

Thirdly, while Strachey generally backed Bevan, their relations were not as close as they had been earlier. This was perhaps because Strachey, as a political economist, enjoyed discussions with Hugh Gaitskell, who became a rising star in the government after his appointment as Minister of Fuel and Power in September 1947. Strachey, no doubt, agreed that Gaitskell was too right wing in his assumptions, but he regarded him as 'formidable', while Bevan was intensely suspicious of him. And there were sometimes new alliances in the government which did not coincide with a Left–Right division. In particular, in the summer of 1949, when there was a severe balance of payments crisis and drain of dollars, it was the younger economic ministers (of both Left and Right) who pressed for devaluation. Gaitskell played a leading role in this, but Strachey was equally clear that it was necessary and, on 26 July, wrote personally to Attlee urging him to devalue before the end of August. (It was, in fact, postponed until 18 September.) Bevan accepted the arguments for devaluation but was not actively involved in the campaign within the government.

Overall then, if Strachey was generally on the Left of the comparatively narrow spectrum of opinion represented within the government, he was by no means a dissident and worked without friction with those who might have been regarded as political opponents. He shared the anti-Communism which increasingly became an integral part of the government's collective mental outlook, talking of the 'degeneration and barbarisation' of Communism.[5] He was also now fervent in his commitment to promote change through the institutions of liberal democracy, arguing that Labour's reforms, and particularly the creation of full employment, meant that: '... one has been able to feel the re-absorption of the working masses into the community, the healing of the incipient schism in the body politic'.[6] All this showed that Marx had been wrong in seeing revolution as inevitable for, he now argued: '... the essence of true statecraft [is] ceaseless, timely adjustment of the institutional framework to suit the changing social content'.[7] He believed that the government was doing just this.

It was thus clear that Strachey's revolutionary days had passed, and he was now prepared to describe himself as a 'staid old middle-of-the-road reformist'.[8] However, this was not the impression created by the right-wing press. For he was forced to spend much of his time as a minister warding off attacks which often used his past record to undermine his current policies.

A controversial minister

Strachey was effective as Under-Secretary of State for Air – having so recently been in the RAF himself, he understood the issues, had a mastery of detail, and was able to present information and policy on matters such as supplies and demobilisation with authority. However, the policy was neither particularly controversial nor very central to government strategy. Therefore he welcomed the opportunity when Attlee offered him promotion to the position of Minister of Food at the end of May 1946.

In general, he was to be competent and energetic, and handled complex issues of supply, price movements and monopolies efficiently. He played an important role in reducing Britain's dependency upon scarce dollars for imports of foodstuffs and gained respect within the Civil Service and government for such work.

John Strachey

He also maintained good relations with the Parliamentary Labour Party. However, public perception of Strachey was dominated by two issues on which he was mercilessly attacked: rationing and 'groundnuts'.

There was, in fact, an overwhelming case for rationing in the general conditions of post-war scarcity. Nor was it resented as much by the working classes as by the middle classes, since many poorer families were gaining in comparison with pre-war conditions and regarded the policy as fair. However, opponents of the government were not interested in its rationale: they wanted to mobilise support with propaganda about 'state control' and the follies and evils of socialism.

Attlee had thus presented Strachey with one of the most difficult posts in the government, without even offering him a cabinet post which would have given him greater control over the policies he was called upon to defend. He realised the difficulty almost immediately and wrote to Attlee at the beginning of July 1946 urging him either to include him in the cabinet or to 'find someone else who you do feel that you can put in the Cabinet, for the job'.[9] However, the attitude of Hugh Dalton, then Chancellor of the Exchequer, to Strachey was quite straightforward: 'Once a Communist, always a Crook.'[10] Dalton probably influenced Attlee in declining Strachey's request, and the Prime Minister somehow managed to head off his resignation threat. In fact, the dispute did not end there and Strachey was later allowed to attend cabinet meetings regularly (unless specifically asked not to do so), and sometimes he spoke on matters outside his immediate area of responsibility. He also became a member of the cabinet's Production and Emergencies Committees (both established in 1947), but he was never granted cabinet rank. This meant that, both in the cabinet itself and in the all-important Economic Policy Committee, his actual status was that of being 'in attendance' and his contributions carried less weight than those of full members.

His problems began immediately after his appointment as Minister of Food. There was an acute shortage of dollars (meaning a restriction of imports), a reduction in world grain supplies and Britain was still responsible for maintaining food supplies in its zone of occupation in Germany, as well as relieving famine in India. The issue of the day was therefore 'bread rationing' – something that had never been introduced during the war. At first, Strachey accepted the need for this but, at the last minute, he came to believe that increased Canadian stocks might make it unnecessary. He convinced Herbert Morrison, the deputy Prime Minister, that a new cabinet meeting should be held and Attlee reluctantly agreed to this. However, the Prime Mininster refused to change the earlier decision, arguing that rationing was a necessary insurance policy. He added that he:

> ... fully recognised the burden this would entail for the Minister of Food and he was confident that all his colleagues would give the Minister their support in the discharge of his difficult task.[11]

This was little more than a sop to Strachey's feelings. It was, in fact, left to him to 'sell' the rationing of bread and other foodstuffs to the House of Commons and the public. He therefore soon became the butt for criticism, consumer protests and popular jokes. During the 1947 fuel crisis, the cry was 'shiver with Shinwell and starve with Strachey' (Shinwell was then Minister for Fuel) and in the popular radio comedy show, ITMA, he was portrayed by Tommy Handley as 'Mr Streakey'. He was one of the most visisble targets for press attacks, with writers implying that he was personally and deliberately making the public suffer for doctrinaire reasons, and his inter-war writings were quoted as evidence against him.

The irony is that, while vehemently defending rationing in public, Strachey was constantly trying to induce the cabinet to implement a less restrictive policy. Perhaps this was motivated in part by the fact that it was he, above all, who was at the sharp end of public criticism. But it was also because he was convinced that more flexibility was both economically possible and politically necessary. For example, he submitted a very long and detailed paper to the Economic Policy Committee in September 1948 in which he argued that food shortages were the privation most acutely felt by the public and:

> If by misapplying our productive effort, we force them to take less food and more radio sets, television sets, household appliances and non-food commodities as a whole, we shall not escape their well merited disapproval.[12]

At various stages he had to fight to prevent rations from being diminished still further but, from 1948 onwards, he secured some abatement in the stringencies of the system (bread rationing ended in July 1948). Even so, rationing was still a dominant theme at the 1950 General Election.

It is a moot point whether Strachey was right, on economic grounds, in believing that the controls could have been reduced earlier. However, the issue was probably not decided so much on the merits of the case as on his relatively junior position in the hierarchy. Douglas Jay recalls that Strachey's long economic memoranda alienated other Ministers,[13] and the decisions were really taken by Sir Stafford Cripps. The latter was so ascetic himself – 'a teetotaller and a vegetarian . . . [who] would rise at 4.00 am and then do three hours' work, before taking a freezing cold bath to stimulate himself for the hard day's slog. . .'[14] – that he was unlikely to be receptive to demands for increased rations, however good the arguments were.

In general, then, the public image of Strachey in these years bore little relation to his actual role in the government. For he was constantly urging the cabinet to bring its priorities more closely in touch with those of 'ordinary people'.[15] However, if the general perception of Strachey was totally unfair on the issue of rationing, the 'groundnuts controversy' was more complex.

The 'groundnuts affair' was a failure, (though not nearly of the magnitude implied by opponents of the government) and Strachey cannot be exonerated from a share of the blame.[16] The enterprise began in March 1946 when the United Africa Company (part of Unilever) proposed to Ben Smith, Strachey's predecessor as Mininster of Food, that a vast area of East Africa, then Tanganyika, (2.5 million acres) should be cleared and planted with groundnuts. Unilever's interest was commercial, but it wanted state involvement to bear the development costs. The rationale put to the government was that Britain was likely to face a permanent shortage of fats unless some such scheme was carried out. Both Smith and the Secretary of State for the Colonies, Creech-Jones, were enthusiastic, and a commission under John Wakefield, and ex-director of agriculture in Tanganyika, was sent to carry out a feasibility study.

The commission reported on 20 September 1946 and recommended a still larger project. It proposed the clearing of 3,210,000 acres (approximately the size of Yorkshire), mainly in Tanganyika, which could produce a minimum of 600,000 tons of groundnuts by 1950–51 at a total capital expenditure of 24 million pounds. By now Strachey was Minister of Food and, on 31 October, he and Creech-Jones submitted a joint memorandum to the cabinet. They argued that more time was needed before embarking on the full scheme, but they proposed an initial small-scale development so that a crop might be obtained early in 1948. The cabinet authorised this but Dalton, then Chancellor of the Exchequer, imposed two conditions: (*i*) that responsibility for the project would be undertaken by the Ministry of Food; and (*ii*) that the crops would be available for British use and not merged into an international pool.

By December, the section of the Ministry of Food which had carried out the investigation, following the October cabinet meeting, issued its report. This broadly endorsed the conclusions of the Wakefield Commission, although an appendix by two scientists predicted some difficulties. On 13 January, Strachey and Creech-Jones went back to the cabinet to seek authority for the full scheme. Strachey admitted that there was an element of risk involved, but argued that this was less than the alternative of not seeking some such new source of edible fats, since supplies of margarine in Britain might otherwise be insufficient by 1950. Creech-Jones expressed more words of caution but supported the proposals, claiming that 'the Departments had taken great trouble to secure the best advice obtainable'.[17] With Dalton also declaring his satisfaction that the balance of argument was in favour (again specifying narrowly British requirements as the main concern), cabinet authorisation was granted for the full ambitious scheme.

From the arrival of the advance party in February 1947, the scheme ran into numerous difficulties: hard soil, inadequate equipment, machinery break-downs, strikes and inefficient accounting systems. The result was that 7,500 acres were planted in the first year (rather than the target of 150,000 acres), and there was little accurate information on costs and machinery stock. On 19 January 1948 Strachey reported to the cabinet that progress had been slower than orignally envisaged and that it would not be until 1949 that the scheme would make an appreciable contribution to the requirements of oils and fats. Costs would also be higher as a result of increases in world prices. This did not, however, daunt him as he confidently asserted that revenues would also be above the original estimates. The cabinet shared his optimism, believing that 'an encouraging start had been made on the project.'[18]

It was, perhaps, perfectly reasonable to believe that, so far, there had merely been 'teething problems' and to insist, as did the White Paper, 'that the first year's operations had not disclosed any fundamental faults in the fundamental conception of the scheme'.[19] However, Strachey had made a major mistake in his choice of chairman for the new public corporation, the Overseas Food Corporation (OFC), which was to co-operate with the United Africa Company for a few months and assume executive control in April 1948. He wanted someone committed to the project, to the notion of a public corporation, and, indeed, to a Labour government. He, therefore, chose Leslie (Dick) Plummer, who was at that time Assistant General Manager of much of the Beaverbrook press. This was an odd choice since Plummer was not an agronomist (although he was a part-time farmer) or an African specialist. But the real problem was that he was also a personal friend whom Strachey had known since their ILP days in the 1920s, when Plummer had been the business manager of the *Miner* and Strachey had edited it. The choice was not 'corrupt' in any normal sense, since Plummer took a reduction in salary and ended a lucrative career, presumably because he was committed to the task he was offered. But if things went wrong, Strachey might now confuse – or appear to confuse – his loyalty to Plummer with his responsibility as a minister. And things now went very wrong.

Throughout 1948 the difficulties accumulated: there was little rainfall, the equipment could not deal with the compacted soil, many Africans lost interest as few social and educational services were provided for the local population, and conflicts within the OFC grew. By September all the heads of department engaged in the project complained to the resident member of the OFC about impractical targets, wishful thinking and remote decision-making, and called for reforms. In October he flew back to London with a new plan, which was broadly accepted. At a very late stage in the year the target for acreage to be cleared in 1948 was reduced from 150,000 to 49,620.

By now, discussion about the whole scheme in London was becoming overlaid with partisan controversy. The Conservatives were aware of the set-backs and conflicts in East Africa and began to use the problems for propagandist purposes against the Labour government in general and Strachey in particular. His reaction (and that of Plummer) was to express an unrealistic optimism and, under increasing pressure, to treat all critics as traitors.

In January 1949 the heads of department submitted another memorandum to Plummer, complaining of endless changes of policy and a situation in which 'we cannot be sure that any decision taken to-day will not be cancelled next week'.[20] Whether or not this was Plummer's fault is uncertain for the objective situation was clearly very difficult, with drought and famine in the first quarter of 1949. (The original commission had probably overestimated the average rainfall.) But whoever was responsible for the local difficulties, Strachey now compounded the problems by refusing to face them.

By March 1949 it was clear that the cost of the revised plan would exceed by far the original authorised expenditure, and Strachey now asked Cripps for more money. He refused and this made the OFC's plan totally impracticable financially (even if it were technically possible). Yet in the House of Commons debate on 14 March, Strachey still sounded wildly optimistic claiming that, on a 'hard-headed' business approach 'the revenues of the scheme ... may well add up to anything up to twice the original estimate' and that 'our scheme ... will be far more needed and far more profitable than was estimated originally'.[21] However, he was vague about the size of the area which would ultimately be cleared and did not inform the Commons that the original plan had been revised downwards. Then, in November 1949, the first annual report of the OFC was published, with strictures on the balance sheet by the auditors. The matter was due to be debated by the Commons and, in addition, both Plummer and Strachey had had to accept a further sharp downward revision of the target acreage to be cleared (from the 3,210,000 originally targeted to 600,000). It was estimated that even this would require a further capital outlay of 16 million pounds up to 1953–54. All this required further cabinet discussion and authorisation. Furthermore, Strachey now wanted to change the board of the OFC by replacing two existing full-time members and hiring two additional part-time business advisers. He saw Attlee before the cabinet meeting and convinced him of the need for these changes to the board, which were then endorsed by the cabinet on 14 November. Detailed research would be needed to ascertain whether there was any valid reason for the dismissals, but at the time they appeared vindictive. For the two men dismissed were Wakefield, who had chaired the original commission; and John Rosa, a banker, who had recently recommended a scaling down of the project.

At the cabinet meeting, Strachey, who was still strongly supported by Creech-Jones, secured acceptance of the new plan, although he now openly stated that no assurance could be given that the scheme would be able to make a profit, even on current account, after the development period. By now, however, more ministers were expressing doubts about the project and Strachey and Creech-Jones were instructed to admit to the House of Commons that grave mistakes had been made and that: '... it would be neither accurate nor expedient to suggest that the Overseas Food Corporation or the government itself were free from blame in this matter'.[22] Strachey was, thus, under pressure within the government as he faced the Commons.

The Conservatives were unsuccessful in their call for an inquiry but made vast political capital from the affair, emphasising 'socialist waste' and the supremacy of private enterprise. But much of the attack was targeted at Strachey personally, particularly for defending Plummer and making scapegoats of those dismissed. Once again, his past political affiliations were used against him and both the *Economist* and *The Times* called for his resignation. Nor was this the end of his agony.

In the course of the Commons debate, he claimed that in June he had personally interviewed all the senior members of the executive staff and had ascertained that they continued to have confidence in Plummer. As soon as this statement became known in East Africa a new furore broke out, which meant that Strachey had to fly out secretly in December to calm the situation. While there, he was explicitly told at a formal meeting that there was a widespread lack of confidence in Plummer.

Before anything further was done to resolve the situation, the General Election took place. Attlee removed Strachey from his position and Maurice Webb, his successor at the Ministry of Food, soon dismissed Plummer. However, it was too late to save the project, as morale plummeted and other senior executives resigned. On 7 December, Webb informed his colleagues that he was abandoning the project. As originally conceived it had, he asserted, been a 'costly failure' (subsequently estimated to have cost 31 million pounds).[23] The OFC had now reached the conclusion that groundnuts could not be farmed in East Africa on a commercial basis and that there was no hope of obtaining any significant supply of oil seeds.

There is no doubt that the 'groundnuts affair' had a major adverse impact on Strachey's reputation. Its immediate result was his effective demotion by Attlee after the February election, whereas he would otherwise almost certainly have been promoted. But it also had a long-term effect so that, when he died in 1963, many obituary writers were more interested in recalling groundnuts than in discussing his theoretical contributions to socialism. This was, of course, absurd and reflected the success of a contemporary right-wing campaign to exaggerate the importance of the affair once it became clear that it was an area on which the government was vulnerable. Yet Strachey certainly made mistakes (in addition to those already mentioned), though some of them were shared by the government as a whole.

First, there was his total enthusiasm and commitment to the groundnuts scheme, once he had decided to go ahead with it. This led him to disregard contra-indications about the viability of the project and, no doubt, the more the Right scented a political scandal and pressed home their advantage, the more utopian and unrealistic he became. It is true that Creech-Jones was normally as enthusiastic as he was and that he was also receiving highly optimistic reports from Plummer. But in view of his general tendency towards a total commitment to the things in which he believed (as previously with Mosley and then the Communist Party), it is probable that his enthusiasm carried others along. As the difficulties mounted, he stopped looking at the evidence objectively. Thus, even after Webb had dismissed Plummer, Strachey maintained that he had 'put up a magnificent performance' and that the scheme would 'still prove of great value to the world'.[24]

The second major failure (which was not his alone) stemmed from a lack of clarity about the original purposes of the project. This had been evident at the first cabinet meeting at which it had been discussed, and had never been resolved. The issue was whether it was seen as a development project which would help the East African economy and pave the way for ultimate independence, or whether it was primarily a commercial venture for the benefit of the British domestic economy. Creech-Jones had seen it in the first sense, but the cabinet as a whole (and particularly the Treasury ministers) were only interested in the narrowly British angle. Strachey secured cabinet backing by appealing to domestic self-interest, although he also shared Creech-Jones's ideals and mobilised wider support for the project on this basis. However, this confusion of aims increased the pressures on the project: had it been seen primarily in terms of the needs of the East African economy then, in theory at least, if the groundnut scheme itself proved impracticable, a new facet of development could have been initiated. As it was, it would be viewed as a 'failure' if it proved unprofitable. In the event, it was only when it failed in commercial terms and the opposition was mounting an attack on it, that the cabinet argued that: '... its merits should not be judged solely by reference to its ultimate capacity to earn a profit'.[25] Strachey was as guilty as anyone for this confusion of purpose. Years later he justified the project in terms of an: '... elementary duty to undertake development schemes in the colonies and ex-colonies, even when the chance of any financial return is small, if we are ever to repay the massive financial support with which the colonies have furnished us.'[26]

But in 1946–47 he had not secured cabinet approval for the scheme on the basis of development. It is, of course, true that it would never have been approved by the cabinet had it been regarded as a development project, and Strachey could perhaps draw a crumb of comfort from the knowledge that East Africa had gained a little from it (though only about 7 million pounds). However, it is extremely unlikely that he had deliberately used the domestic economic argument to secure cabinet approval, while actually being more concerned about African development. In fact, he had probably hoped, without much analysis, that Britain and East Africa would benefit equally. If so, he was guilty of the kind of muddled thinking that he would have condemned in his theoretical works.

The outcome of the 'groundnuts affair' was a personal blow and humiliation. However, Strachey remained generally enthusiastic and optimistic about the achievements of the government.

At the time of the February 1950 General Election, he wrote:

> Hitherto it has been the 'inarticulate major premise' ... that the sole two existing modes of existence for advanced industrial communities were (i) capitalism, with, typically though not universally, a democratic political superstructure, or (ii) a fully socialised economy, catastrophically instituted and with a fully dictatorial political superstructure conducted by a Communist Party along Stalinist lines. We now know that it is, demonstrably, possible to begin, and to carry at least some little distance, the process of socialisation ... by the methods of Parliamentary democracy.[27]

And a few months later he remained confident that the government could move forward towards socialism, 'even while a decisive part of the means of production remained in private hands.'[28]

In fact, Attlee's second Labour government was to be far more difficult that the first and, by October 1951, Strachey would be much less confident.

The second government (February 1950–October 1951)

Even before the General Election, it had been evident that the government was now more concerned to defend its record against Conservative promises of 'freedom from controls' than to offer any further radical advance. Nevertheless, the new administration, with a much reduced overall majority of five, started easily enough with a stable economy and relative confidence and unity around a programme of consolidation. However, Strachey's own position remained difficult.

In his post of Secretary of State for War, he was under Shinwell, as overall Secretary of State for Defence, and again without cabinet rank. This was disappointing for reasons of status and also because it removed him from the economic sphere in which his primary interests lay. Nevertheless, he was philosophical about his new job and anxious to play a constructive role in the government. However, it was at this time that the first major post-war spy scandal broke, with the prosecution of Klaus Fuchs, a government defence scientist, as a Communist agent. On 2 March the *Evening Standard* published the following headline: 'FUCHS AND STRACHEY; A GREAT NEW CRISIS. War Minister has never disavowed Communism. NOW INVOLVED IN MI5 EFFICIENCY PROBE.' And the charge was taken up by the other Beaverbrook papers.

This was deeply painful for Strachey, who was just recovering from the press hounding over the 'groundnuts affair'. The break with the Communist Party had itself been traumatic; to face public attack ten years later was scarcely less difficult. Nor was Attlee very much help, for he and Shawcross (the Attorney-General) dissuaded Strachey from instituting criminal libel proceedings against the Beaverbrook press. Instead he was forced to make a humiliating public statement, itemising details of his relationship with, and attitude to, the Communist Party since 1940. It was left to Michael Foot and *Tribune*, rather than Attlee and the cabinet, to defend Strachey (as a result *Tribune* faced a costly action in the High Court).

This had scarcely subsided when Strachey once again precipitated further attacks upon himself by launching a vehement condemnation of Schuman's proposal for a coal and steel community. This time, as he himself admitted, the row over his speech was largely his own fault. There was never the remotest chance that the Labour government, which had been wholly negative about all proposals for supranational integration since 1948, would join a coal and steel community. Strachey could, therefore, have relied upon the relevant ministers to have rejected the proposal in the most diplomatic terms possible. Instead, he criticised it in strident terms, thereby provoking another well-orchestrated outcry from the opposition (which did not really want Britain to join a coal and steel community either). This then meant that he was forced to make a further embarrassing statement, apologising for the tone of some of the expressions he had used. He had made his intervention because he felt so strongly on the subject (see Chapter 6), but his action unnecessarily annoyed Attlee, who had to agree to a special House of Commons debate on the speech. All this meant that Strachey was in a comparatively weak position within the government as it faced the major crisis of the era: the Korean War.

When North Korean forces crossed the 38th Parallel and invaded the South on 25 June 1950, there was little sign that the unity of the government and party would be destroyed. There was no dissent within the cabinet – and virtually none within the party – from the orthodox, simplistic, pro-American perspective. In other words, it was generally agreed that this constituted North Korean aggression at the behest of the Soviet Union as part of its crusade for the worldwide expansion of Communism. Nor was there any doubt in the minds of ministers that a firm Western response to this aggression was necessary. The cabinet, therefore, backed the Americans in legitimising their own military entry into the war by securing United Nations' endorsement for the action (and, in fact, fighting on behalf of the United Nations). Within a few months, the cabinet also willingly agreed to send British troops to help the war effort.

During the next six months, however, tensions – and ultimately splits – occurred on three issues, all resulting from American pressures: first, a demand for massive British rearmament; secondly, a simultaneous insistence on German rearmament; and finally, the apparent American wish – personified by General MacArthur – to extend the war by invading China and possibly using atomic weapons. While all these caused great conflict within the cabinet, it was the defence commitment, and its domestic impact, which precipitated the political crisis for, in April 1951, it led to Bevan's resignation from the cabinet, accompanied by

Harold Wilson. (John Freeman, a Parliamentary Private Secretary also resigned).

Bevan had been sceptical about the increased defence programme the previous August, arguing that the best method of defence against 'Russian imperialism' was improvement of the social and economic conditions of countries threatened by Communism.[29] Then on 25 January 1951, when the cabinet very reluctantly accepted a defence budget of 4,700 million pounds over a three-year period, he had condemned the impact of the defence programme on the economy and had been sceptical about the alleged military threat. However, he clung on until Hugh Gaitskell (now Chancellor of the Exchequer) imposed charges on dentures and spectacles to help pay for the rearmament. As the resigning ministers made clear, their action was not simply because of the imposition of charges on the National Health Service (NHS). It was also because the pace of rearmament was seen as unrealistic in view of shortages in raw materials and machine tools, and would undermine the goals of government economic and social policy. Nevertheless, for Bevan, the architect of the NHS, the attack on the principle of free health care was the acid test and a resigning issue. He was also quite right in regarding it as a complete irrelevance in comparison with the expenditure committed to rearmament: it raised a paltry 13 million pounds.

Strachey had long discussions with Bevan at the time, and many believed that he might also resign. Why did he not do so? In order to answer this question, his general attitudes to the manifold crises associated with the Korean War must be considered.

As a defence minister, Strachey did not dissent from his military advisers' general assessment of the need for rearmament and the probability of imminent war with the Soviet Union. Indeed, there was no sign that he dissented from the hypothesis, on which the Chiefs of Staff were authorised to work, that war was 'possible in 1951 and probable in 1952'.[30] He also shared the cabinet's wilingness to use military measures in the struggle against Communism. In July 1950 he went further and faster than Attlee in proposing that British forces in Hong Kong should be 'offered' to the Americans in Korea.[31] It is possible that, having so recently been accused of being a Communist, Strachey was demonstrating his 'Western' credentials. On the other hand, the fact that he was still suffering from his past associations may have led him to project his anger and frustration on Communism, thereby making his current antipathy to it particularly vehement. In either case, it meant that his attitude to 'Communist aggression' in Korea was quite in line with that of the government as a whole. Nevertheless, Strachey was a dissident within the admininstration from the autumn of 1950 until April 1951.

His most fundamental concern was that American foreign policy was aggressive and provocative, and that it would be disastrous for Britain simply to follow the lead of the USA. While he had no doubts about the Korean War itself, he always feared that the American action might lead to a generalisation of the conflict, involving war with China. One of his primary motives in suggesting the involvement of British land forces in July 1950 had, therefore, been the hope that this would give Britain more influence over American policy.

By the winter of 1950–51 he had become almost obsessed with the danger that the Americans would precipitate a new world war either by generalised conflict with China or by insisting on German rearmament even if the Soviet Union made concessions. Between January and April he therefore wrote a series of memoranda to Attlee and other cabinet members insisting on the paramount need for Britain to dissociate itself from American policy, and to adopt an independent line, irrespective of the possible reactions of the American government. His possibilities of influencing the cabinet were reduced by the fact that he was no longer present at the meetings. He therefore needed to work through Shinwell, who did not share his views. This may have made Strachey's tone still more fervent and desperate, leading Gaitskell (who saw the maintenance of close Anglo-American relations as the overwhelming priority) to regard his anti-Americanism as 'almost pathological'.[32]

In fact, Strachey mounted forceful arguments against the military necessity for German rearmament and denounced the view that the government should not enter into serious negotiations with the Soviet Union lest this lessened tension and thereby undermined public support for rearmament. Underlying this, and many of his other representations to the cabinet, was the belief that:

> It is surely no overstatement to say that war with China and Russia during 1951 or 1952 would involve not the risk but the virtual certainty of national disaster for Great Britain. Let us face the simple, military fact that it is probable, almost to the point of certainty, that this country cannot physically survive a third world war which begins before land and air forces which can prevent Russia occupying the Channel coast have been created.[33]

The danger in the Far East seemed still more immediate and, after many pleas for a change of policy, Strachey wrote a top secret letter to Shinwell on 6 April 1951, claiming that MacArthur was deliberately engineerng a totally catastrophic general war with China, and that Britain must now tell the American government that it could no longer countenance the use of British forces under his command.[34] Almost immediately afterwards, the American government finally dismissed MacArthur.

Strachey had not been alone in his views. The question of German rearmament had divided the cabinet completely, and Attlee had only been able to secure support for the principle by postponing its implementation to the indefinite future. And the majority of the cabinet were alarmed by the American extension of the Korean War into China and the apparent threat to use atomic weapons. Attlee had even flown to Washington in December 1950 to attempt to induce the American government to adopt a more cautious policy. But, as usual, Strachey saw the issues in 'life-and-death' terms, whereas others may have been less exercised about them. This made the dismissal of MacArthur particularly important to him, for he was ready to believe that it presaged a new development in the international policy of the USA, and that unity of purpose between the two governments would now be restored.

However, the date of the dismissal was also of great significance in relation to Strachey's attitude to Bevan's resignation. For MacArthur was removed at precisely the same time as Bevan was deciding whether to resign over Gaitskell's budget. It is not clear whether Strachey would have resigned over the government's attitude to American foreign policy, but he was obviously acutely worried about it and, in these circumstances, may have considered resignation when Bevan finally decided to go. Certainly, his opponents in the government hoped and believed that he would do so. But the dismissal of MacArthur — and the shift in American policy that this seemed to imply — would inevitably change his attitude to Bevan's resignation. This can be appreciated if his view of the specific issues involved is now considered.

A notable feature of Strachey's position was that, from the start of the Korean War, he had realised that rearmament expenditure would mean that other aspects of the government's programme would be deleteriously affected. On 23 July 1950, less than a month after the war began, he had publicly stated that defence expenditure meant a diversion of resources from 'the productive and constructive tasks on which the Nation has made such wonderful progress in these brief five years since the last

War'.[35] Other ministers had not wanted him to state so openly that defence expenditure would detract from economic reconstruction because Attlee had not yet said anything about this. Strachey had kept the reference in his speech because, presumably, he regarded it as important to make the point explicitly. Yet he was prepared to maintain whatever defence expenditure was necessary to fight the war.

Although he was sceptical about the practicability of the 4,700 million pounds rearmament programme that the cabinet adopted the following winter, he maintained the logic of the position that he had outlined in July. Having accepted that the attempt must be made to finance rearmament, he was also prepared to accept Gaitskell's measures. Afer Bevan resigned, he thus told Attlee that:

> I have throughout the crisis considered the imposition of the charges in teeth and spectacles to be a mistake, but have also considered – and still consider – this issue by no means large enough to make one resign rather than accept a Cabinet decision. And I have made this position clear to both Aneurin and the Chancellor.[36]

A few days later he justified his stance to his constituents. Arguing that it was regrettably necessary to hold down social services expenditure, he continued:

> But if you agree that the amount of money being spent on the social services, had, this year, to be limited, then I do not know that this particular way of dealing with the Health Scheme was worse than the other alternatives, such as reducing hospital facilities and the like. For my part, I cannot regard this issue as by any means a resigning matter.[37]

He accepted that the resignations had also been on the wider issue of the rearmament programme, but claimed that it was too early to tell what level of rearmament was physically possible. Given his stance on the Korean War and the need for rearmament, and his reassurance about American policy following the dismissal of MacArthur, this was a perfectly logical line to take.

Nevertheless, Strachey's failure to resign was highly significant. Twenty years earlier, when he and Bevan had been very close to one another politically and personally, he had chosen to leave the Labour Party, while Bevan had remained within it. This time it was Strachey who remained the 'insider' (and, indeed, he may have been influenced to stay with the government on this occasion in reaction against his years as an 'outsider'). But once again, Bevan's political instincts and deeper roots in the working class gave him a surer touch. Without yet offering a fully coherent rationale, or even acting particularly consistently, he clearly felt that it could not be right to hit working class living standards in order to finance a massive rearmament programme to fight an American-led anti-Communist crusade. Strachey tried to maintain a logical position but, in deferring to the advice of the military establishment and the authority of the cabinet, he had made yet another political choice: he would not become a 'Bevanite'.

Although the resignations did not lead to open conflict within the party until after the October election, they fatally weakened the government. It appeared to lose all its confidence, and some of its key personnel. It now rested on a record which no longer appeared so positive, as the pressures of rearmament and war partially eroded the bases of the welfare state. Strachey sensed this. By July, he was effectively endorsing Bevan's case by suggesting to Shinwell that the rearmament programme should be backed by mandatory priorities and controls but phased over a longer period so that it 'would both get us more genuine armed strength and impinge less on the civil economy'.[38] More generally, he feared that the Korean War had unleashed a right-wing backlash and that:

> we are entering a period when merely to stick to the simple, basic

> traditions and beliefs of Socialism will be almost more difficult than it has ever been ... The very success which we have had, the very progress towards Socialism which we have made, have inevitably created counter pressures and resistances perhaps more formidable – certainly more subtle – than those with which our Movement has ever had to struggle.
>
> Those pressures are playing upon us both in the economic and in the political field. Our whole social and economic environment is still predominantly capitalist; and it is all the time consciously or unconsciously seeking to bend and twist us back towards the old world.[39]

Indeed, he now appeared so pessimistic about the achievements of the government that Attlee commented that a draft of the above speech could be interpreted as saying: '... that only Bevan and Co. are keeping the true faith and ... the rest of us are being led away. This should be corrected.'[40]

Attlee believed that Strachey was exaggerating the impact of the war, particularly when he argued that it was reversing the steps towards greater economic equality which the government had achieved. In fact, Strachey was quite justified in this belief for, while austerity measures hit working-class living standards, company profits soared by over 25 per cent between January and August 1951 in the boom created by the Korean War. But although he sensed the loss of direction, he was not at all sure what should be done about it. He was clear that nationalisation must continue, but not at the same pace as it had between 1945 and 1948. He believed that the party should experiment with new forms of ownership, industrial democracy and decentralisation, but had no immediate concrete proposals. He was convinced that the government had established the kind of managed economy that he had envisaged in 1940, and that this was a supremely important achievement. But he now thought Labour would need to be 'conservative' in maintaining these gains and that the essential message was 'to stick like grim death to the things we believe in'.[41]

In the last few months of the Labour govenment, Strachey was acutely conscious of the fact that the initiative was being lost and that there was a danger that the achievements of the first five years were being threatened. But he reflected the malaise that he observed, for he had no real idea as to how the next stage of socialism could be implemented. The Labour government had effectively run out of steam and was now on the defensive. There was, therefore, something symbolic in Attlee's decision to hold a General Election in October, primarily out of concern for the King's failing health.

Although the Labour Party lost this General Election (despite winning more votes than the Conservative Party), Strachey was not too disappointed. For some time he had been collecting material for the writing that he had been unable to do while in government, and he was now looking forward to this. Despite his energy, efficiency and enthusiasm, he had not been a success as a minister. To some extent this was because he had been vilified by the Right for much of the time. Attlee himself – perhaps belatedly – recognised this when, in December 1951, he wrote to thank him 'for all the good work you did': 'You had a very hard task at the Ministry of Food and have had to sustain a bitter campaign of calumny which continued when you went to the War Office.'[42] But it was also because his enthusiasm sometimes outweighed his judgement. He was no longer the same person who had acted as Mosley's lieutenant in the second MacDonald government – both because he had learned his lesson and because he was far more sympathetic to the administration's general policy. But he was still impatient of cautious bureaucratic obstacles and constitutional conventions: when he believed something, he wanted to be able to act on it himself or to influence others into sharing his views imediately. Sometimes he was justified in this, as he almost certainly was in urging greater flexibility over rationing in the late 1940s, and a more independent foreign policy in 1950–51. On other occasions – and most notably over the 'groundnuts affair' – his over-eagerness led to problems. But this total commitment to the things in which he believed was embedded in his character and was the simultaneous source both of his strengths and weaknesses.

After 1951 he would never again be a government minister, but he had learned a great deal from the experience and from his closeness to crucial developments in the establishment of the post-war settlement. Once the Labour Party went into opposition, he would try to explain what he had learned, not by reminiscences, but by attempting to understand the possibilities of reformist socialism in a theoretical context. Involvement in the Labour government was perhaps to lead to his most important work of all: his attempt to understand post-war capitalism.

6 *Contemporary Capitalism (1951–1956)*

From the loss of the General Election in October 1951 until the next election nearly four years later, the Labour Party was deeply divided. These conflicts were evident at every conference as majority opinion in the constituencies moved to the Left while the Right remained dominant within the Trade Union movement. In Parliament the ideological conflict, which underlay the division, was reinforced by the personal antagonism of the two main protagonists – Gaitskell and Bevan – whose personalities seemed to symbolise two contrasting visions for the party.

Both sides emphasised the achievements of the 1945–50 government, but the Bevanites believed that the movement had lost its way when it had opted for 'consolidation' and had played down its socialism. What was required, they claimed, was a reaffirmation of traditional socialist values, reflected in domestic policy by further nationalisation; and, overseas, by a far greater independence of the USA, a reduction in defence expenditure, and a more positive social and economic policy in the Third World. Perhaps the most emotive issue in the Bevanite opposition to the leadership was over the question of German rearmament, which was seen as a means of consolidating the European division when it might be transcended, increasing the risk of war, and tying Western Europe to American strategic and political demands. The Right of the party was generally united in opposition to these policy demands (with a few exceptions on the issue of German rearmament), although there were some important differences within this camp. One strand, symbolised by older stalwarts, such as Herbert Morrison, was generally content to oppose the Conservative government by defending the record of the Labour administration, without much sign of creative thinking about the future strategy of the party. The second group of younger figures, amongst whom Gaitskell was pre-eminent, shared many of the political inclinations of the older Right – particularly their fervent anti-Communism and Atlanticism – but was far more active in searching for a new rationale for the party in the changed circumstances of the 1950s. However, the old and new Right co-operated on policy and on disciplinary measures against Bevan and his followers.

In general, Attlee endeavoured to prevent the disputes from tearing the party apart. Nevertheless, in March and October 1952 and in April 1955, he favoured severe measures against the Left for breaches of party discipline and, particularly on the last occasion, Bevan came near to expulsion. (Ironically, within a few months he re-joined the shadow cabinet instead.)

Even before the loss of the 1951 General Election, Strachey had tried to put himself forward as a mediator between the two groups and he maintained a 'centrist' role throughout the period. The only occasion when he was really effective in this capacity was during the first crisis in the PLP in March 1952, when Bevan and over fifty other members of the Left defied the leadership by voting against the government's defence estimates. Attlee and the Right then put forward a resolution which not only proscribed future breaches of party discipline but also referred in emotive terms to past occurrences. Aware that this would be highly divisive and could even drive Bevan out of the party, Strachey successfully led a PLP 'Keep Calm' group to replace this resolution with a more moderate one which referred only to future breaches of standing orders. However, he was out-manoeuvred by Attlee when he tried to repeat this tactic in October of the same year, when the leadership was intent on disbanding the Bevanites as an organised group.

In general, Strachey was not a major influence within the party at this time and was not elected to either the NEC or the shadow cabinet. In the increasingly polarised party, neither side turned to the centre and both Left and Right saw him as 'wibbly-wobbling in the middle'.[1] There was an element of truth in this criticism, for Strachey was certainly finding it difficult to decide between the protagonists. However, he also wanted to promote 'centrism' for positive reasons. This was both to maintain an effective opposition against the Conservatives and because he genuinely believed that it was vital to include both Left and Right within a single movement. He thus regarded Bevan as a 'passionate moderate' whose genius was 'a treasure . . . for the Movement'. But he also argued that the party needed its 'solid strand' and that its periods of strength depended on the two strands remaining 'firmly entwined'.[2]

This outlook made Strachey appear aloof from the passions which animated both sides in the party dispute. And, in a sense, he was. For between 1952 and 1955 he was trying to make sense of Labour's role in the contemporary situation from a far larger historical perspective. And there was a personal aspect in this, for he was simultaneously reviewing his own past as a Communist in the light of his subsequent position as a mainstream Labour politician.

His preliminary conclusions were revealed in four articles for the *New Statesman* in May 1953 under the heading 'Marxism revisited'. These surprised many by the extent to which Strachey – in the midst of the Cold War consensus – was still endorsing a semi-Marxist perspective, and also by his open acknowledgement that there had been only a very marginal redistribution of wealth and income between the social classes in the twentieth century. However, 'Marxism revisited' was only a beginning:

Strachey's real energies were devoted to the book which was eventually to be published as *Contemporary Capitalism* in 1956. In terms of its intellectual content, *Contemporary Capitalism* was probably the most stimulating and important book that Strachey ever wrote. But before its argument is examined, it is worth looking at the work in the context of Strachey's own development.

A typical reaction to *Contemporary Capitalism*, even by sympathetic critics, was to feel that it was detached and intellectual. It is, therefore, significant that he anticipated this reaction and wrote, in an unpublished chapter:

> This book will strike cold upon the imagination of many readers. It cannot gather to its aid the passion and idealism of that revolutionary socialist movement which has existed for the past hundred years within Western society. It has been written in the 'light of common day'.

But, as so often with Strachey, this sober rationality masked some very deep emotions and, although he was now totally committed to a reformist socialist perspective, he looked back at his Communist past with some real regrets:

> The noble dream of perfected brotherhood, security and well-being, abruptly to be realised, here and now, out of the successful revolt of the miserable and the exploited, has been dreamt. It cannot be dreamt again for the sleeper has awakened ...
>
> No-one whoever caught even a glimpse of that vision can deny the sense of loss at its fading ...
>
> ... the glory and the dream of the great revolution of their period will recede. In the light of their common day what is, and what is not, possible for the humanity of their time will become bleakly apparent. For them there will be no occasion for the social-intoxications of the pre-revolutionary period.
>
> Such is the inevitable sense of loss occasioned by the fading of the vision.[4]

If ever an apparently cool and dispassionate book represented 'the strangled cry' of repressed emotion, it was *Contemporary Capitalism*. For Strachey was trying to come to terms with his whole past political life in the light of his present position. The detached tone reflected his painful acknowledgement of the fact that the most creative and exciting years of his life had been based on beliefs that he now regarded as false.

A second significant point about the book is that the published text was far more limited than the earlier drafts. What Strachey had set out to do was to examine the development of capitalism as a whole in relation to his earlier views: for example, to explain why Fascism had developed in Germany but not in the USA and Britain; and to look at the relationship between capitalism and imperialism. The really intensive reappraisal of his beliefs, therefore, took place at this time and formed the basis for the theoretical content of *The End of Empire* (published in 1959), as well as *Contemporary Capitalism*. As Strachey himself said, he put 'everything' into this work.[5] Appreciation of this fact makes it easier to understand the book itself and Strachey's subsequent political development.

In *Contemporary Capitalism*, Strachey was consciously attempting to integrate Marxism into what he termed the 'Western cultural tradition'. It is debatable whether the result was the synthesis he was seeking or an unresolved contradiction, but both influences are clearly present in the work. This meant that it was totally unorthodox in the Cold War climate of the 1950s, even within the Labour Party. Strachey had no doubts that the prevailing system was still 'capitalist', but he believed that it had undergone a mutation in relation to the original species. Amongst the factors which accounted for the difference, the following were the most fundamental to his analysis:[6]

(*1*) that the economy was dominated by a few large units,

which meant that, within limits, managers could control prices and thereby affect profits by conscious decisions;

(2) that state intervention in the productive process occurred so as to overcome the disastrous tendency to instability which resulted from domination of the economy by a few large units. Such intervention operated on the crucial issues of the distribution of income, the level of total demand, the relationship between consumption and investment, the pattern of production and the level of foreign transactions; and it was rendered effective by new methods of national income accounting;

(3) that the power of labour had increased in two crucial respects:

(a) through the formation of effective trade unions able to face employers with some real strength;

(b) by using political influence over the democratic state so as to lead to favourable legislation which further enhanced bargaining power with employers 'by providing the workers with sources of income independent of their employers, in the form of social services, and by full employment policies'.[7]

While Marxists normally termed this system 'monopoly capitalism', to signify their oposition to it, and others called it 'the welfare state', to signify their approval, Strachey's term was the 'last stage of capitalism', suggesting that it was both the latest and ultimate phase: '... it will be succeeded not by a third version of the system but by something which it would be manifestly an abuse of language to call capitalist at all'.[8] Last stage capitalism had two possibilites: if uncontrolled, or controlled in the interest of the oligopolies, it would be far worse than 'the old' capitalism; but if controlled in the interests of the population as a whole, 'it may be superior, both in stability and equity'.[9]

In order to control the economy in this way, there was a series of prerequisites in terms of the level of economic development, and the nature and operation of the political system. But, argued Strachey, it was also necessary to understand the underlying forces at work in a capitalist economy. His explanations and critiques of various economic theories formed a brilliant excursus into the history of economic thought, and Strachey still maintained that Ricardo's contribution was far greater than that of the neo-classical economists, who had led the subject into a blind alley by making assumptions about equilibrium and automatic adjustment which had borne no relation to reality. However, his real concern was with the extent to which Marxist theory still provided the fundamental insight into contemporary capitalism.

Strachey's view of the central issue in Marxist economic theory followed from his long-term political preoccupations: the issue of wages and employment under capitalism. If, as he believed, contemporary reality diverged from that which appeared to follow from Marxist theory, and from his own views in the 1930s, it was essential to explain why.

His intellectual solution to the problem was to argue that there was a confusion of logical-deductive and empirical elements in Marx's original theory. With one half of his mind Marx had simply applied to the determination of wages the general theory that all commodities exchange in proportion to the number of hours of socially necessary labour that they contain. If so, the socially necessary labour which produced the commodity of labour power (i.e., that which the employer buys from the worker in the form of wages) was simply the amount necesssary to sustain the employee and his or her family. From this, it followed logically that wages could never depart substantially from subsistence level.

But the question of whether commodities, in fact, exchange in proportion to the socially necessary labour contained in them was empirical rather than logical, and could not, therefore, be assumed to be true. This was so, both in general and with regard to the specific issue of wage levels. Although he accepted that

Marx's arguments were extremely powerful and less rigid than those of some of his followers, Strachey maintained that Marx's final conclusion (as stated in *Capital*, Vol 1) was that the process of capital concentration would lead to ever increasing misery amongst the workers with a growth in the 'mass of poverty, oppression, enslavement, degeneration and exploitation'.[10] Nor would Strachey accept that the Austro-Marxists were justified in claiming that Marx's real view had been that the workers were exploited by a process of 'relative immiseration' which enabled real wages to rise with increases in production, but by less than the increased share which was appropriated in the form of profits. He saw this as an illegitimate attempt to rescue Marxism by reconciling it with actual developments in the real world.

It was not difficult to show that, in reality, increased 'immiserisation' had not occurred in contemporary Britain, the USA or North-Western Europe. In comparison with the pre-war situation (let alone with Marx's own times), primary poverty had been vastly reduced, full employment with increased wage levels had been established, and the working class could benefit from improved social welfare and educational provision. Where, then, did Strachey believe that Marx had gone wrong?

In his view, Marx was quite correct in analysing the factors in the capitalist system which exert a downward pressure on wages towards a subsistence level. In particular, the dual processes of increased mechanisation, on the one hand, and the growth of the supply of labour on the other, would constantly tend to have this effect. Where Marx made his mistake was in viewing these as 'laws' rather than 'tendencies', for:

> they may, at certain times and places, and under certain conditions, be overcome. In particular they have, quite incontrovertibly, been overcome in . . . advanced last stage capitalism, *operating in a democratic political environment.*[11] [original emphasis]

Nevertheless, the underlying thrust of capitalism as an economic system was exactly in the direction that Marx had analysed. In other words, the economic system itself had an innate tendency to extreme and ever growing inequality, so that all the increases in wealth would – unless counteracted – go to the small class of owners, while wages were held at subsistence level. Even in the democratic advanced capitalist societies, the extent of inequality remained vast and redistribution had been very marginal. The working class, therefore, had 'to run very fast to keep in the same place relatively to the other classes'[12] (through social services, wage increases and redistributive taxation).

Strachey's conclusion from all this was that Marx's economic insight had been correct, but that: 'He failed to see that other, essentially political forces would arise in the advanced capitalist societies which would balance, and, in the end, even begin to outweigh, the inherent tendencies of the system.'[13] What had actually happened was that the weight of working-class interests operating on democratic institutions had modified the operation of the system. The process of working-class enfranchisement and trade union demands had initially forced even pro-capitalist parties to make some response to the needs of the workers. Subsequently, the creation of working-class parties had vastly reinforced the democratic pressures on the system. Paradoxically, therefore, the making of anti-capitalist demands had ultimately 'saved' the system by forcing it to raise the wage earners' standard of life and so prevent polarisation and collapse. And he maintained (against the extreme Left) that this was the right course for socialists to take: the experience of allowing capitalism to collapse, leading to slump and Fascism, had taught socialists that the goal was to supersede the system while enabling it to function.[14] (This was exactly the position that he had taken in the *Programme for Progress* in 1940.)

However, Strachey was not complacent about the extent to which capitalism had been tamed. Democracy, which he defined as 'the diffusion of power throughout the community'[15] was in sharp contradiction with the economic tendency which was strongly inegalitarian and towards the concentration of power. However:

> Such contradictory trends can hardly co-exist indefinitely. One must overcome and absorb the other; for political power and economic power are, in the last resort, merely aspects of one indivisible whole, namely power itself.

And he concluded:

> Economic power threatens to submerge political power unless political power can at the critical moment obtain control of economic power . . .
>
> The democratic forces, using their political power, must be strong enough to bit and bridle the economic power of capital: if they are to succeed, they must know *how* to control the workings of the system while they are transcending it.[16]

Of all the existing mechanisms for operating the economy in the interests of the people as a whole rather than simply in line with the demands of capital, he saw public expenditure and investment as the most crucial. He had no patience with the official Communist view that Keynesianism was economically fallacious, but he thought there was some validity in a more sophisticated Marxist approach which argued that public intervention could not be taken beyond narrow limits because it was in conflict with the interests of the capitalist class. Nevertheless, he saw it as defeatist to believe that this was the end of the matter and: '. . . that, short of the total overthrow of capitalism and the breaking of all capitalist resistance, nothing can be done to which the capitalists object'.[17]

Similarly, it was true, as Communists maintained, that capitalists would accept expenditure in armaments far more easily than other forms of public intervention. But he maintained that the results of Keynesian policies were so attractive to the mass of the population, that even right-wing governments were now forced to maintain them. This led Strachey to an important theoretical conclusion, implicit in the whole book, though he accorded it only the status of a footnote::

> The basic communist error ... derives ... from the Marxist theory of the State. The State, they declare, is nothing but the instrument of the great capitalists. It is inherently incapable of undertaking such activities as the application of the Keynesian techniques for peaceful purposes. If it does apply them, it is bound to apply them exclusively for arms making. Keynes fell into an opposite error. He assumed that the State was just the State, to be controlled presumably by disinterested economists. The fact is that in the conditions of contemporary democracy the State and its vast powers are rather prizes for which all sorts of interests are struggling and competing.[18]

Therefore, so long as effective democracy continued to exist, the electorate could impose Keynesian economic policies, joined with traditional socialist measures of public ownership and social reform, to enhance the position of the working class.

But the transformation of last stage capitalism through democracy was by no means inevitable. The existing balance was unstable and capitalist forces could be expected to try to manipulate, distort and, if necessary, frustrate the workings of the system to their own advantage. Not only was monopolisation of the press a distinct threat to democracy, but increased propaganda against 'the tyranny of the State' was already evident and could be expected to grow.[19] As the top 10 per cent lost control of 'their state', they would seek to undermine belief in that state itself, because it was now responsive to the wishes of wage-earners

John Strachey

But if democratic social change were to be frustrated, this would undermine the countervailing pressures which were indispensable to the present working and future transformation of last stage capitalism. This would lead instead to control on behalf of 'big capital', tipping the balance of the economy into unworkable lop-sidedness and economic breakdown, as in Germany in 1931–32, and would result in totalitarianisim.[20] Strachey did not see this as probable, for the Conservative Party had broadly accepted the change in the balance of power between big business and the wage earners, effected by the previous Labour government. However, he wondered what would happen if serious economic problems forced the government in power either to go further forward or back towards the inter-war position. And what would a right-wing government do after the memory of 1945 had receded? He feared that those whose deepest motivation was to preserve capitalism at all costs might ultimately turn against democracy, which would otherwise prove deadly to their interests.[21]

Strachey was naturally still more concerned with the dilemmas of the Left. The faith of wage-earners in democratic institutions could easily be dissipated unless those institutions were shown to be capable of gradually remodelling society:

> Thus the party of the left must be able, decade by decade, to show a certain minimum measure of economic change, on pain of decay. And this will not be easy. Society is stiff and intractable material on which to work . . . Only powerful and sustained pressure on the part of the party of the Left can re-model it. It is indispensable to such a party to retain a strong reforming zeal if it is to have any hope of success.[22]

In particular, it must not be diverted by anti-Communism into becoming a bulwark of the status quo. Indeed, the sole way to defeat Communism was to bring about the indispensable reconstruction by democratic means. The greater the improvement in the workers' wages, the more they would find that democratic institutions really could be valuable to them. Similarly, their improved economic position would give them access to educational and cultural facilities, thereby increasing their commitment to democracy as a tangible benefit rather than an abstract ideal. For Strachey, everything now depended on 'whether contemporary democracy can be preserved and made into an effective instrument of social transformation'.[23]

Three points about the conclusion of the book are worth noting, for they define Strachey's credo at the time. First, he recognised that his work might be criticised for dealing with the problems of the 1930s that had now been surmounted. But he utterly rejected the view that capitalism had solved its problems and would 'now sail on serenely through the second half of the century'.[24] He agreed that the difficulties were soluble, but was convinced that they would only be solved by:

> mobilising every ounce of economic knowledge, political insight, wisdom and practical skill, which we can command; and then only by means of transforming the very nature of the system, until in the end, it is no longer capitalism.[25]

Secondly, he still believed that Marxism provided the basis for a rational and scientific method which could lead to valid economic discoveries. The dangers were that its conclusions would not be recognised because they threatened class interests; or that its fallibility would lead to the abandonment of reason which could 'plunge us back into an intellectually dark age'.[26] It was the 'cast iron intellectual system' of Communists that had crashed, not Marxism, which should be 'a marvellously flexible method'.[27]

Finally, Western socialists must not allow disillusionment with the French and Russian Revolutions to destroy their ideals. They could not help knowing what catastrophes had followed from the distortions of revolutionary goals, but:

> The ideal of democratic socialism may be thought of as the attempt at length to realise those aspirations in combination; to realise a liberty that will not turn into the liberty to exploit, and equality that will not contradict variety, and a fraternity that will not become its opposite by striving to impose co-operation by force.[28]

Despite the importance of *Contemporary Capitalism*, it certainly contained some weaknesses. There were structural defects in its frequent references to issues that were to be taken up in subsequent works, and arguments were sometimes left incomplete. This was because the original conception was much wider, and it had been necessary to cut the book at the last moment. Nor were all the theoretical problems satisfactorily resolved (probably an impossible task). In particular – as will be discussed further later – the concept of democracy was very restricted, and Strachey's notion of the transformation from last stage capitalism into socialism was never fully explained. Indeed, even his views on the immediate next steps were left very sketchy. These weaknesses were related to some fundamental theoretical problems in his view of the state.

Strachey anticipated a later important debate in Marxist circles by arguing that orthodox Communist theory was defective in its view that the state was simply the servant of capitalist interests. He argued instead that the state could become – and was becoming – the instrument of wage-earners and could, therefore, fundamentally change the social and economic structure. As he put it, he had come to believe that the superstructure could transform the economic base, and now felt that the orthodox emphasis on a one-way determination from base to superstructure was misconceived. But just how much autonomy did the state have in relation to the predominant capitalist interests? And how exactly did the wage-earning majority push their demands when these conflicted *fundamentally* with the interest of capital? These problems are crucial to the whole issue of whether socialism can be established peacefully, but Strachey hardly addressed them. His explicit formulation of the state as an arena in which all sorts of competing interests operate and attempt to make their will prevail came very close to a 'pluralist' perspective. But this was negated by his belief in a fundamental conflict within society which must ultimately be resolved by the predominance of either economic (anti-democratic) or political (democratic) power.

There was a further, related weakness at the heart of his whole theory of social change. Strachey's fundamental explanation for the relative progress of the working class was that its pressure, operating through a democratic political system had led the state to adopt policies which ran counter to capitalist economic logic. Even if this is accepted – and Strachey's own analysis suggested that other factors were also at work – what reason was there to believe that this pressure would continue to be sufficient to maintain the impetus in the future? The effects of electoral competition to secure reliable Conservative support amongst the working class did not constitute 'pressure' to transform the system towards socialism. This would presumably depend upon the extent of working-class radicalism, but Strachey believed that the militant mood had passed. If so, he either needed to argue that further socialism would come about in a deterministic fashion through the operation of the system itself, or that the mood would again change. But he appeared to believe neither of these propositions. Since he also realised that 'oligopolistic' control of the press could further undermine the post-war consensus, and that there were powerful anti-democratic forces within capitalism, his apparent confidence was unexplained. If, as he argued, the existing settlement was temporary and reflected the balance of forces established by the war, what reason was there to assume that it would be succeeded by a more, rather than a less, progressive one? In other words, Strachey did not really even provide a convincing account of how 'last stage capitalism' would be maintained, let alone how it would be transformed into socialism.

Yet even to discuss these problems in the late 1980s shows the prescience of the book. For Strachey was writing in the era of the 'affluent society', when most commentators were convinced of the long-term stabilisation of capitalism. It was hardly surprising that he too tended towards a degree of complacency. But, unlike the majority, he recognised the vulnerability of the post-war settlement and the conflicts which lay just below the surface. Furthermore, he feared that once economic instability recurred, particularly as the memory of 1945 receded, conservative forces could attack the basis of the modified capitalist system: arguing that 'the state' was a threat to 'liberty', they might seek to limit its role, thereby reducing the extent to which it represented the interests of wage-earners, and recovering it as their own instrument. Few could have predicted the nature of 'Thatcherism' with such deadly accuracy.

A further criticism that can be made of *Contemporary Capitalism* is that it was vague about the immediate measures that a Labour government would need to take to move towards transformation of the system. This was partly because the purpose of the book was theoretical/historical rather than practical. However, Strachey himself had intended to include one specific set of policy recommendations which he believed to be crucially important. The reasons for his last minute decision not to do so are of great interest.

At this stage, Strachey remained totally convinced that it was imperative to safeguard economic sovereignty. In addition to his general belief that this was essential for the maintenance of full employment and other reformist goals, he was adamant that a government of the Left needed additional controls. Above all, he argued that any left-wing admininstration which tried to implement a mildly progressive programme would be threatened by a flight of capital which could make the implementation of the domestic reforms totally impossible. The essential prerequisite of socialist measures such as public ownership and redistribution, was, therefore, a foolproof system of controls over foreign exchange, capital movements, imports and exports so that the domestic programme could be safeguarded against the attempt to send capital abroad.

For Strachey, this was no side issue, but was central to the politico-economic strategy to which he had adhered since 1940 when he had come to believe that it was possible to implement a progressive programme without revolution. It was largely this convinction which had led him to take such a strong and undiplomatic stand against the Schuman Plan in 1950.[29] Furthermore, in the process of reviewing the past when writing *Contemporary Capitalism*, he now came to believe that this was the crucial issue for democratic socialism. It was, he claimed, the discovery that 'even the smallest steps forward by a reformist, social democratic government produced an economic crisis' which had led to the despair of gradualism by 'many of us' in 1931. This had seemed to be triumphantly refuted by the 1945–50 Labour government, but he now thought it evident that this success had been made possible because that government had inherited a system of wartime controls indispensable for success. Since many of these were no longer available, the precondition for further successful reformist socialism was the application of new controls.

In February 1954 Strachey wrote an article in the *New Statesman* in which he expressed all these views.[30] He maintained that, unless the arguments were stated explicitly now, neither the leadership nor the party would be prepared, when elected, 'for the formidable job' of imposing the controls. This would not only mean deceiving the electorate but would lead to a catastrophic failure when the attempt was made to implement the programme.

> the life or death of British social democracy depends upon this issue. In my humble opinion it far transcends in importance even the question of how much more nationalisation we ought or ought not to do. For we shall never have the opportunity either to nationalise a single industry or to do anything else, unless we have faced up to the question of how we are to carry on the economic system in the meanwhile.[31]

The article provided Tory ammunition that a Labour government would reimpose unpopular state controls, and Gaitskell (the shadow Chancellor) expressed annoyance at the intervention. But Strachey was unrepentant, telling Gaitskell that the issue was paramount, that it would be disastrous to court electoral popularity at the cost of electing a 'disarmed, impotent Labour government', and that Gaitskell should make a public statement in favour of the necessary controls even though this would lead to inevitable attacks by the Tory and City press.[32]

Gaitskell remained totally unconvinced by the argument and certain that Strachey's article would lose votes. Nevertheless, the latter returned to the subject in a draft chapter for *Contemporary Capitalism*. He now broadened the controversy:

> Behind the view that this whole issue is 'too hot to mention' lies a strange hope in certain democratic socialist hearts that it will somehow be possible to 'creep up' upon the capitalist system and transform it out of existence without anyone noticing ... Such democratic socialists feel that all would be well if only the fools, knaves, or extremists in their own party would keep quiet. This sort of thing might perhaps be a harmless delusion if it did not lead straight towards that atrophy of the will, and that decomposition of the body, of democratic socialist parties, of which history affords

the most alarming examples.

The essence of his case was:

> that the socio-economic nature of last stage capitalism is such that there exists a sort of 'social ejection mechanism' which, unless its operation is foreseen and neutralised, will ruin governments of the Left. In Britain this mechanism usually takes the specific form of a tendency to recurrent balance of payments crises. British democratic socialist governments must be able to take control of the balance of payments of their country from the outset. For if they cannot, they will be quickly bankrupted by the efflux of liquid capital seeking what it considers to be more attractive conditions.[33]

Apart from his admitted preoccupation with the experience of the 1929 Labour government, Strachey's argument was rooted in his Marxist assumptions. For him, it remained axiomatic that there was a fundamental conflict of interest between capital and labour, which meant that any attempt by a Labour government to improve the relative position of wage-earners would almost certainly lead to a flight of capital to areas where wage levels were lower and the return on capital was higher. If, on the other hand, a democratic socialist government imposed the necessary controls on foreign transactions, these – coupled with the ability to reflate the economy if faced with a domestic 'go-slow' by private investors – would mean that: 'it would have achieved the power progressively to remould the economy to any desired extent'.[34]

Strachey thus argued that there was a confusion between two views about democratic socialism. The first, which he held himself, was that it was possible progressively to transform the capitalist system, ultimately out of existence, democratically and without provoking the violent resistance of the holders of capital. The second was the illusory view that this could be done without losing the confidence of capitalists, or even with their approval.

Yet this was the underlying assumption of all those who supposed that it was unnecessary for a Labour government to provide effective controls over foreign transactions.

Strachey was not advocating a radical advance to socialism: once a Labour govenment possessed the necessary power it could act with 'discretion and forebearance', without pushing economic change at such a pace that the fabric of society could not stand the strain. The controls were simply the prerequisite for moving towards democratic socialism and thus avoiding the 'almost equally repulsive' alternatives of uncontrolled capitalism or Stalinist Communism.[35]

He no doubt oversimplified the purely economic problems involved in a government attempting to control the economy when large-scale capitalists were wholly antagonistic to its policies. And he did not tackle such issues as political destabilisation at all. Nevertheless, his argument that a democratic socialist government proposing mildly radical measures was liable to precipitate a flight of capital was theoretically sound, and was subsequently to be reinforced by the experience of the Labour governments in the 1960s and 1970s and the French socialist government in the 1980s.

There is firm evidence that Strachey maintained these views after the publication of the book.[36] Why, then, did he not include what he described as his 'principal economic conclusion' of thirty years in the labour movement,[37] in the published version? The reason was, almost certainly, that Gaitskell again objected to Strachey publishing his viewpoint. Whereas in 1954 this had not been sufficient to deter Strachey from putting forward the argument, the difference was that in December 1955 Gaitskell became leader of the party. Although the final proofs of the book were ready to be sent off for printing, Strachey gave Gaitskell time to read them and all the evidence suggests that he cut out the argument about controls because he did not wish to alienate the new party leader.[38] This leads to the paradoxical conclusion that *Contemporary Capitalism* would have contained a more practical policy recommendation had Strachey only been a theorist rather than combining this role with that of practical politician.

Contemporary Capitalism was generally well received; it was translated into numerous languages and was discussed by the Left on both sides of the Iron Curtain in Europe, in Asia (selling 10,000 copies in Japan alone) and in Latin America. However, it did not quite make the impact for which Strachey had hoped in the USA and Britain. In the former, this was scarcely surprising for, as his publisher pointed out, works which were critical of capitalism were simply viewed 'with suspicion that amounts to fear'.[39] Nevertheless, it was greeted enthusiastically by many left-wing intellectuals: C. Wright Mills, for example, told Strachey that it was a 'model' for the kind of book that he would like to write himself.[40] Its reception in Britain was more complex.

It would be quite wrong to imply that *Contemporary Capitalism* was not welcomed within the Labour Party. On the contrary, it was widely acclaimed as a highly important work at the time of publication, and is still often discussed in studies of British socialist thought. But although it certainly had some influence over younger intellectuals in the party, it never became a 'bible' for any sector of the movement. In his review of 'socialist literature in the fifties', Bernard Crick was, therefore, justified in claiming that, although *Contemporary Capitalism* was as important a work as Crosland's *The Future of Socialism*, it was not read nearly as much.[41] This coupling of Strachey's work with Crosland's, which was published later in the same year, provides a clue to the latter's greater popular success, but not for the reasons normally given. It is often suggested that the two books were very similar but that Crosland's was more readable, wider in scope and more 'committed'. Both are, therefore, cited as 'revisionist' texts, but Crosland's is seen as the more important work and, therefore, understandably, the 'text' for the Gaitskellites.[42] However, Crosland and Strachey were saying substantially different things.

The Future of Socialism became the source book for the revisionist Right in the Labour Party because it explicitly stated that traditional forms of socialism offered no help in defining the goals of the contemporary Labour Party. Above all, this was because, in Crosland's view, the system was no longer 'capitalist': it was a 'mixed' economy in which most of the goals desired by the Labour Party had already been attained, in which managers were now motivated by fundamentally different goals from capitalists and in which class differences were largely subjective rather than objective. If this society was no longer 'capitalist', it followed that the Labour Party need not be 'socialist' in any conventional sense. Most goals could be achieved by the continued operation of the existing economic system at a high growth rate, and with reforms such as the introduction of comprehensive education to bring about greater equality of opportunity. Crosland was the Labour theorist *par excellence*, who was arguing that the problems of economic instability had been overcome and that society was now characterised by consensus on the post-war reforms. And his message was absolutely clear: the Labour Party should abandon the grandiose visions, which were now irrelevant as well as electorally damaging, and concentrate on necessary reforms.

Certainly, there were overlaps between the two books but Strachey's stress on the enduring fundamental conflict in society, the precarious nature of the settlement, and the need for reforming zeal and understanding by the Labour movement differed very substantially from Crosland's emphases. Strachey wrote as a revisionist Marxist who wanted to demonstrate that it was possible to reform and ultimately transcend capitalism through a system of parliamentary democracy. Crosland wrote as a revisionist-Right member of the Labour Party who wanted to convince the rank and file that they should abandon Left-Labour policies and concentrate on piecemeal reform. Strachey himself had no doubt that there were important political differences between the two works, as was clear from his review of *The Future of Socialism* in the *New Statesman*.

After some general praise, he attacked the book from a Left perspective. Whereas Crosland believed that ownership of the means of production was irrelevant, Strachey maintained that it was the most important single determinant of social structure and that social ownership was the only permanent basis for a classless society. If socialists ever lost sight of this, they would cease to be socialists at all and would 'subside into the role of well-intentioned, amiable, rootless, drifting, social reformers'. Furthermore, by implying that those dispossessed of their class privileges would not resist, Crosland – like Bernstein before him – was probably a 'hopelessly premature optimist' and, if he was wrong, 'his book may lull us into neglecting precautions which could avert catastrophe'.[43] (This was probably a further reference to the necessity for economic controls.)

But if *The Future of Socialism* was the text for the revisionist-Right in the Labour Party, *Contemporary Capitalism* could hardly serve as a source of inspiration for the Left. Strachey's interpretation of Marxist economic theory, in general, and relative and absolute 'immiserisation', in particular, elicited some interest amongst the more independent Marxist economists, and led to renewed correspondence with Maurice Dobb, with whom Strachey had had little contact since 1940. But although many Marxists took his economic analysis seriously, the political message of the book was so restrained that it was hardly a source for revolutionaries: it was, in the words of one Indian Communist reviewer, more a halfway house 'for those tired of the journey'.[44] Nor was it a book for the Labour Left, who were, in general, scarcely more interested in Marxist economic theory than the Labour Right, and found it difficult to respond to a work which failed to offer any concrete suggestions on the burning controversies of the day.

The fate of *Contemporary Capitalism* was, therefore, paradoxical: it was probably the most original, thoughtful and mature of Strachey's books, but it was also the one with the least political resonance in any section of the British labour movement. Nevertheless, its completion was a cathartic experience for Strachey himself. He had relived his Communist years in the process of writing the book and had come to conclusions about 'last stage capitalism' which he was never again to re-examine in any depth. He now wanted to believe that these issues had been resolved and that he could work within contemporary capitalism rather than theorise about it.

The position which he had adopted throughout this period, both in his writing and his political life, had been 'centrist': that Bevanites and anti-Bevanites should stop 'knocking hell out of each other' and concentrate on the real issues.[45] But once he had relived the possibility of capitalist collapse and justified a reformist solution to his own satisfaction, it was inherently unlikely that he would maintain this position. It was more probable that he, like the capitalist democracy about which he had written, was in a state of precarious balance, liable to move to the Left or to the Right. By 1956, newly appointed to Hugh Gaitskell's front bench as one of the defence experts, all the signs were that it would be to the Right.

7 The rational anti-Communist (1956–1963)

From 1956 until his death seven years later, at the tragically early age of sixty-one, Strachey remained on Labour's front-bench with responsibility for various aspects of defence until 1962, and subsequently for Commonwealth affairs. Although he was never one of Gaitskell's inner group of confidants, he became increasingly influential, particularly on defence policy on which he was, by 1963, acknowledged as an expert on both sides of the Atlantic. He also achieved a reputation in many parts of the Commonwealth in which he travelled widely, and particularly in India where he stayed as a guest of Nehru shortly before his death. By now, he was one of the most experienced politicians in the Labour Party and would almost certainly have been Commonwealth Secretary in the Wilson government elected in October 1964.

Despite his front-bench responsibilities, he was also extremely productive in research, writing and lecturing in these last years. His major achievement was probably *The End of Empire*, published in 1959 as the second part of a trilogy on democratic socialism. Like *Contemporary Capitalism*, this was translated into many languages, and discussed in both developed and Third World countries. Moreover, unlike *Contemporary Capitalism*, it had particular resonance in Britain for, at a time of rapid decolonisation, its theme was that it was both possible and desirable to survive without an Empire. The third part of the trilogy, *On the Prevention of War*, was published three years later and was, once again, reviewed and discussed widely, though far more outside the labour movement than within it.

These major works were complemented by a series of shorter writings and lectures, of which the best known was *The Strangled Cry*, originally published in *Encounter* in 1960 and reissued with some other essays in 1962. This was a long essaay on anti-Communist literature, dealing with Koestler, Orwell, Whitttaker Chambers and Pasternak. Here, Strachey criticised the form of anti-Communism which renounced reason itself because of the Communist appropriation of rationality. Against this he set forth his own, purportedly rational, critique of Communism. In this, his style was at its most powerful and incisive, and he demonstrated a rare ability to combine political and literary sensitivity. The essay was, therefore, received with acclamation amongst the liberal intelligentsia in many countries. Finally, he gave a series of lectures, setting out his last views on the relationship between political and economic systems;[1] he reconsidered the role of Lenin;[2] and he was writing his reflections on historical and current events when he died.[3]

Strachey's energy and ability to combine politics and writing, remained remarkable. However, there was a marked change: after 1956, and particularly in the last three years of his life, Strachey moved steadily to the Right. Indeed, his shift in position was probably as extreme as in any other of the various phases of his political life, although it was less noticeable since he remained on Labour's front-bench and did not announce any doctrinal conversion. The political manifestations of the change were, nevertheless, evident. Whereas he was still a 'centrist' in 1956, by 1963 he was one of the principal opponents of the Labour Left on the revisionist-Right of the party. This was reflected in his attitude to the two major political conflicts within the party in these years: the controversy over 'Clause 4'; and the battle over unilateral nuclear disarmament.

When Labour lost its third successive General Election in 1959, Strachey did not believe that Gaitskell was well advised to provoke internal conflict by attempting to revise Clause 4 of the party's constitution. He thought that this kind of overt attack on the commitment to public ownership was tactically inept and he made these views clear to his leader. However, he himself argued that the lesson of the defeat was that a 'new kind of social democracy':

> will have to be designed to appeal to people who are not in active revolt against their conditions of life. Therefore, it is bound to be less militant, more liberal in the philosophical sense of that word, and less strident, in the tone of its propaganda.[4]

He was, thus, sympathetic to Gaitskell's attempt to 'modernise' the party by changing its image, even though he disagreed with him tactically. Of far greater importance to him, however, was the issue of unilateralism, on which he had no disagreement with his leader. When a unilateralist motion was passed, against the wishes of the leadership, at the 1960 Labour Party Conference, Strachey backed Gaitskell's campaign to reverse the decision the next year. He participated actively in the movement to bring this about, speaking and writing in favour of 'multilateralism' and, in this context, he became a vice-president of the Gaitskellite Cambridge University Social Democratic Society. He now saw the 'modernisation' of the Labour Party and the defeat of unilateralism as the same battle and, when Gaitskell died in January 1963, Strachey paid tribute to 'his courage and colossal effort' in bringing about victory on both fronts.[5] Indeed, by then, Strachey appeared more revisionist than Gaitskell himself, for he had joined the group of fervent pro-Europeans, round Roy Jenkins, who were alientated by Gaitskell's nationalistic speech at the 1962 Party Conference, and he had become a devotee of American nuclear deterrence theory.

This shift in political position was naturally reflected in his theoretical work. Apart from *The End of Empire*, which was very well received in the Labour Party, Strachey's subject matter and approach now tended to please Ango-American liberals and alienate the traditional Labour Left. This was also evident in his choice of outlets, for he became a frequent lecturer and contributor to American-financed anti-Communist organisations, such as Radio Free Europe, *Encounter* and the Congress for Cultural Freedom. The transformation was symbolised by his deliberate decision to break with Gollancz, who had published all his work since *The Coming Struggle for Power*. He prepared the ground for this by allowing The Bodley Head to publish *The Strangled Cry*, but the real reason was that he did not want Gollancz – now a pacifist – to be associated with *On the Prevention of War*.

This separation from his past political associations was not easy for him. When he severed his connection with Gollancz, he told him:

> I have just as profound an admiration as ever for your life-work and all it has meant. And just as much gratitude for all you have done for me.
>
> But I feel that ... pacifism ... is the thing you now care about more than anything else in the world. I have come to the other conclusion ... Therefore the 'break' has, in that sense, tragically but inevitably, already happened. For the real character of our relationship as author and publisher was that we believed in the same things.[6]

Moreover, his change in perspective also affected his domestic life, for Celia sympathised with CND and could no longer accept or understand his opinions.

He made some new political friends on Labour's right-wing and in 'Atlanticist' circles, but these could not replace those that he had lost. In his last years he was thus a rather lonely figure

The rational anti-Communist

– alienated from the Left and yet still very different from most of the Revisionist Right. But for Strachey, ideas remained of paramount importance and, once he had formed his opinions, he would not compromise. Let us, therefore, now look at his writings in this period, before attempting to explain his final political evolution.

The first notable point about his ideas is that there was no sharp break with his past beliefs. In particular, Strachey never renounced Marxism, although his version became increasingly sanitised, diluted and idiosyncratic. By the 1960s he could thus write:

> I am still enough of an old Marxist to suppose that only neurotics could become communists at the moment, because the objective conditions are so unpropitious. Capitalism is working so incomparably better than any of us supposed it ever would. However, probably I do not, as usual, allow enough for irrationality.[7]

While a Marxist might have agreed that the most appropriate policy in a non-revolutionary situation was to press for reforms, Strachey's position was different. He was, in effect, claiming that, because capitalism was stable, support for even the notion of revolutionary transformation was irrational.

Nevertheless, he remained committed to the view that Marxist theory provided the key insight into capitalist development, particularly in emphasising the relationship between the economic base and the superstructure of ideas. However, whereas until 1956 he had used revisionist Marxism to demonstrate his belief that socialism could be brought about peacefully, by 1963 he was invoking the name of Marx to uphold the status quo and denounce Communism.

The End of Empire represents a transitional phase in this movement from the centre to the Right of the Labour Party. Much of it was completed by 1955, but it was then rewritten to focus more specifically on the issue of imperialism, following a trip to India during the following year. Work on it was temporarily interrupted in the winter of 1957-58 when Strachey suffered from a heart attack, and it was finally published just after the 1959 General Election. It was an ambitious book, with historical and theoretical analyses of the causes and effects of imperialism, and it contained some of Strachey's finest historical writing. Its major purpose was complementary to that of *Contemporary Capitalism*: it was to demonstrate that advanced capitalist economies in democratic societies did not 'need' imperialism to sustain their economic development. Once again, this was an integral part of revising orthodox Marxism-Leninism and the beliefs that Strachey had held in the inter-war period. And the argument was also essentially similar: whereas Lenin had been fundamentally correct in believing that the imperialism of 1870–1914 had arisen because of the falling rate of domestic profit, once the problem of 'ever increasing misery' had been resolved the drive towards imperialism could be (and had been) transcended because the domestic market could offer a sufficient outlet for profitable investment. Nor was the possession of an overseas empire necessary to sustain a high and rising standard of living at home for, he argued, it was domestic economic policy and the post-war changes in the relationship between the state and the economy which were overwhelmingly responsible for increased living standards. While finance capitalists might make super-profits from overseas investments, the real economy would benefit far more from the domestic use of these surplus funds.

The attempt to demonstrate that imperialism was neither necessary nor advantageous for advanced democratic capitalism was one major purpose of the book. A second crucial aspect was a passionate plea for the transfer of resources from the wealthy to the less-developed countries in order to make their economic development possible. Relying largely on work by Gunnar Myrdal,

Strachey explained how the operation of market forces simply widened the gap between rich and poor countries. He, therefore, combined a moral appeal to end world poverty with the argument of enlightened self-interest – that this was the only way to maintain the operation of the world economy. All this foreshadowed the Brandt Report more than twenty years later and was expressed at least as eloquently. Strachey was also prepared to admit that the post-war Labour government had continued the exploitation of poor countries in the Commonwealth (by using their sterling balances to reduce Britain's dollar gap) and that this increased the particular duty for Britain to undertake development schemes.

The book was received enthusiastically by both the Left and Right of the Labour Party because these arguments were in harmony with contemporary thinking. The notion that the British Labour Party could act as a bridge between the 'first' and 'third' worlds in a multiracial Commonwealth was at its height. *Tribune* devoted a whole page to the book, proclaiming that Strachey had identified the mission for the party and that *The End of Empire* should be read by everyone;[8] and other Labour Party reviewers were scarcely less enthusiastic. In general, the book appeared politically fairly similar to *Contemporary Capitalism* and more relevant to current perceptions of contemporary issues. However, there were some signs of a rightward shift.

First, the anti-Communist theme was now more pronounced. Beause Strachey wanted to refute the Communist view that capitalist countries could maintain control of less-developed states wihout the need for formal empires, he tended to ridicule the argument without adequate discussion. His own definition of imperialism was very narrow and enabled him to let the USA (and Britain) off lightly for maintaining 'informal' control in the Third World, while indicting Soviet hegemony in Eastern Europe. This anti-Communism was also evident in his discussion of decolonisation, where he justified repression when the alternative would be to hand power to Communists, and questioned whether independence should be granted to Communists or pro-Communists even when they had been elected democratically.

Secondly there were signs of a significant change of emphasis in his attitude to the relative importance of politics and economics, both historically and in the contemporary world. While he did not understate the economic damage that Britain had caused its Empire, he revealed pride in its record of political admininstration and in establishing the basis for representative institutions, particularly in India. And he now argued that, in Britain, a new sense of national purpose, outside the economic system, was necessary to put in the place of the Empire.

The downgrading in the importance of economics and reverence for political institutions, coupled with anti-Communism, were to be highly significant in Strachey's last years. In *The End of Empire* these themes were not prominent (perhaps partly because the theoretical work had been finished four years before the book was published), but they were to become increasingly dominant in his other late writings.

These signs of a shift in position were consolidated into four major elements in these works: a more complacent attitude to the capitalist economy; an increasingly liberal emphasis on political institutions; a pervasive and profound anti-Communism; and a growing preoccupation with the 'threat' of unilateralism. These can be illustrated briefly.

Although Strachey never renounced the theoretical position that he had set out in *Contemporary Capitalism* he now took economic stability for granted. He no longer emphasised the inherent conflict between political democracy and capitalist oligarchy, or the need for further socialist transformation to ensure the triumph of the wage-earners. Instead, he implied that the battle had already been largely won and that the political institutions and economic system were now in harmony. This did not mean that Strachey – any more than Crosland – claimed that no radical change was necessary. But it did mean that he assumed that the system was broadly satisfactory and that there was no need for any fundamental modifications in the foreseeable future.

This declining radicalism was particularly evident in his attitude to economic inequality. Whereas in the early 1950s he had stressed the limitations of the changes which had been achieved in the distribution of wealth and income this theme was hardly present in his later work. It is true that he continued to express a personal belief that large-scale hereditary wealth should be ended or greatly modified, but he no longer regarded this as a burning issue, and postponed it to the indefinite future when the British electorate became conscious of the issue. His more immediate feelings about the subject were implied when, in 1958, he wrote that: '... to reopen the social conflict by suggesting a more equitable distribution of the national income is an uninviting prospect from which it is not necessarily craven to shrink.'[9] By 1963 this relatively honest attitude had been replaced by the far more conventional apologia for capitalism that there was, in fact, considerable equality, and that redistributive taxation had made a vast difference in this respect.[10] This was a total reversal of his earlier position both on inequality in general and on the specific inefficacy of taxation as a means of redistribution. Nor did he now argue that public ownership was the sole means of creating further equality and ending hereditary wealth.

A similar shift was evident in his attitude to political institutions. Even in *Contemporary Capitalism* his concept of democracy had been a very narrow one. In essence, it comprised the traditional liberal notions of universal suffrage, an independent judiciary and a free press, supplemented by trade union rights and political competition through a two-party system. As long as there was genuine competition between two parties (made possible by a free flow of information), he argued that governments and would-be governments would be forced to make concessions to the working classes in order to secure their votes. In an indirect, but real, sense the wage-earners would, therefore, rule.

Strachey had thus advocated an 'elitist democracy' in which the electorate made its political choices by voting and then left it to governments to carry out their policies. Although he had defined democracy as 'the diffusion of power throughout the community', there was no discussion of mass participation through demonstrations, strikes or local action groups. Even though his concept of democracy had been so restricted in *Contemporary Capitalism*, his principal purpose had been to demonstrate that capitalism could be *transformed* through democratic means. Subsequently, the transformative element all but disappeared.

By 1958, he was arguing that the main function of a democratic system was to 'mediate' between conficting social interests and he maintained that election results provided sufficient evidence of what wage-earners 'wanted'.[11] Five years later he claimed that:

> the establishment, preservation and development of democracy . . . rather than the question of what kind of economic system is best, has now become the main question in the public life of the world.[12]

Since he now regarded democracy as an end in itself rather than as the best means of bringing about social transformation, the restrictiveness in the original concept appears even more unsatisfactory. The ultimate goal thus became the preservation of the poliltical institutions of liberal democracy and, indeed, in some unpublished work, Strachey even stressed the advantages of constitutional continuity.

The other side of this was Strachey's increasingly bitter

condemnation of Communism. Even in the early 1950s there had been a close relationship between Strachey's limited concept of democracy and his anti-Communism. In *Contemporary Capitalism*, for example, he explicitly argued that his model was not to be measured against some abstract ideal but against the alternative — party dictatorship. However idealistic were the motives of Communist leaders, their attempt to rule though party dictatorship was bound to lead to physical violence and mental constraint because there was no 'mechanism by which their populations can modify, control, or periodically change, their governments'.[13] Precisely because they were irresponsible, they failed to reflect the complex, ever changing, reality of highly developed modern communities, so that their decisions began to lose touch with reality and, ultimately, could be imposed only through coercion. The supreme negative value of democracy was, according to Strachey, that it prevented governments from implementing policies to which the people were fundamentally opposed.

Yet, at this stage, Strachey had at least believed that the *goals* of Communism and democratic socialism were similar, even though the difference in *means* was supremely important. But as his attitude to economic transformation and liberal democracy became less radical, his anti-Communism became more fervent. In his last years, Strachey became increasingly preoccupied with Communism, in general, and the Soviet Union, in particular. He tried to provide a theoretical basis for his views (in addition to the general emphasis on the importance of democracy) by developing an argument that he had begun in 1940.

The fundamental Communist mistake, he claimed, lay in the belief that certainty was possible in the social sciences. This was an intellectual error, for none of these sciences was nearly sufficiently developed. But it was the underlying cause of all the tragedies of the Communist world for:

> the fact is that Communists are absolutely convinced that *they* always know best; that they know much better than the masses themselves what are their true interests.[15]

Given this conviction, the 'Party' is endowed with divine right and this 'has led, and still leads, to crimes and disasters seemingly without end'.[14]

In his final published work, he went still further, arguing that, in their conviction of certainty, Communists:

> have crashed forward over mountains of corpses, over the suppression of even the most elementary human liberties, over a wider area and over a longer period, and with a greater completeness than the human race has known, at least for many centuries.[15]

From this he drew the implausible conclusions that, had the Mensheviks triumphed in 1917, Russia would by now probably have been a social-democratic state; Hitlerism may not have triumphed (because the German Left would not have been divided); and both the Second World War and subsequent Cold War could have been averted.

Strachey may have tried to differentiate between his form of anti-Communism and that which was 'irrational' and total, but it is not clear that he succeeded. His attitudes to capitalism, democracy and Communism were obviously very closely interrelated. At first sight, his position on defence would appear quite separate. There are two reasons for this: first, unilateralism has never been a typical Left/Right issue because there are CND supporters who do not take a left-wing stance on other matters; secondly, Strachey's attitude to defence was constant. During the Second World War he had believed that the bombing of German cities was justified if this led to victory, and he now claimed that nuclear weapons were a necessary part of Western strength. In both cases, he assumed that the fundamental moral questions were involved in the choice of ends – anti-Faacism or anti-Communism – rather than in the means to these ends. He had, thus, supported the development of nuclear weapons throughout the post-war period, and now became partisan because of the politicisation of the issue rather than through any change in his own views. Despite these differences between defence and the other issues, however, Strachey's stance against unilateralism undoubtedly constituted the final major element in his shift to the Right.

One reason for this is that, within the Labour Party itself, unilateralism became a Left/Right division, even if this was less apparent in the country as a whole. As already noted, Strachey saw the issue in this way and came to believe that the defeat of unilateralism was a necessary prerequisite for the 'modernisation' of the party. But, of still greater relevance, was the fact that he was not merely a 'multilateralist' but a leading light in the anti-CND activity, who believed that the maintenance of a bipartisan defence policy was the supreme question in contemporary British politics.

Specific evidence of the way in which defence policy reflected the rightward shift in his thinking can be seen in the following attitudes and assumptions. First, Strachey frequently denigrated the motives, stability and intelligence of CND activists, while praising Pentagon strategists as sober, reasonable people, whose deterrence theories provided the best short-term guarantee for the avoidance of nuclear war. Secondly, he ultimately abandoned all vestiges of his former belief that war was rooted in particular economic or social systems, and claimed that the nation-state itself caused the expansionist drives that led to war. And thirdly, he now maintained that the best hope for the future lay in the recognition by the super powers of two common interests: the need to avoid nuclear war; and the wish to maintain their world ascendancy by ensuring non-proliferation.[16]

Strachey had some foresight in perceiving that limited disarmament might come about when the super powers believed this to be in their interests. On the basis of this assumption, he was a strong advocate of the Test Ban Treaty, which was signed just after his death, and might be credited with predicting some of the forces which led to later arms control agreements. But his notion of a world hegemony or condominium for the super powers and limited sovereignty for all other nation-states was hardly a progressive idea. Nor could his rather superficial attempt to argue that the ultimate solution lay in world government make it much more attractive. And, despite his apparently even-handed treatment of both super powers, his fundamental motivation in defence was anti-Communism. This was evident both in his frequent denunciations of unilateralism as a recipe for surrender to Communism, and in his willingness to accept a doubling of Western defence expenditure rather than tolerate any retreat in the face of Soviet power.[17]

Thus, by the end of his life, Strachey had become a left-of-centre, pro-Western, anti-Communist politician on the revisionist-Right of the Labour Party. How is this shift to be explained? One contemporary answer by Richard Crossman, a fellow Labour politician and intellectual, was straightforward and unsympathetic. In his view, there was a tension in Strachey between the theoretician and the ambitious politician, and the latter finally triumphed.[18] In other words, Strachey was corrupted by his ambition to achieve high office in a government led by Hugh Gaitskell, and adapted his outlook accordingly.

It is true that Strachey was as ambitious as most politicians, and he certainly looked forward to a cabinet position in the next Labour government. And yet it is highly unlikely that this was the fundamental reason for the shift in his view. Had ambition for high office been a dominant character trait he would not have acted as he had at decisive stages in his career. He would probably never have joined the Labour Party in 1924, for there were more conventional routes for him to have taken to achieve power. But, having joined, he would never have cast himself into the political wilderness (as he knew he might be doing) in 1931. It is true that throughout his career he had enjoyed being at the centre of things – and this had even been true when he had been an 'outsider' with Mosley or the Communists. After 1956 he therefore appreciated his position on the front-bench. It is also evident that there could be tensions between his writing and his political career, and it may be that Strachey sometimes compromised on his theoretical integrity when there was an overt clash between the two – as he had done by omitting a section of *Contemporary Capitalism* (see chapter 6). But this is very different from suggesting that he would fundamentally alter his political perspective because of a burning ambition. Ideas were so important to him – indeed his whole adult life was so bound up with a passionate search for a valid theory – that an opportunistic shift in outlook seems wholly out of character. Nor could it even account for some of his actions. For example, in late 1962 when Strachey was alienated by Gaitskell's conference speech on the EEC, he wrote to him to condemn his action. This was not the most effective way to curry favour with the party leader.

A second interpretation, favoured by many of his colleagues on the front-benches and, no doubt, by Strachey himself, was of 'intellectual conversion': that is, that in his final years he was persuaded by the force of the arguments and evidence to adopt the perspective of the revisionist-Right of the Labour Party. This explanation is also unsatisfactory. Few would accept the suggestion that any socialist position is *solely* a matter of theory, evidence or logic: values, goals and subjective experiences are also involved. In Strachey's case, we have continually seen that, despite his own emphasis on rationality, his emotions were always crucially important in accounting for his political perspective at any time. Indeed, his search for valid theories often emanated from a need to provide a satisfactory intellectual underpinning for a belief that he had already come to hold. This was at least as true in the last years of his life as it had been earlier.

If neither ambition nor ideas in themselves can account for the shift, the real explanation lies in a complex interaction between Strachey's own circumstances and character, and the wider intellectual and political context of the time. Although Strachey's shift in position was not caused by intellectual conversion *per se*, it is, nevertheless, evident that one crucial change in theory enabled him to adopt a more right-wing theoretical framework. This lay in the economic sphere.

For more than thirty years, Strachey's principal political preoccupations had centred on fundamental issues concerning the capitalist economy. At all stages, his political position had been tied up with his beliefs as to whether or not capitalism was susceptible to reform. As we have seen, when he wrote *Contemporary Capitalism*, he was still convinced that the economic system was prone to instability largely because of its fundamental inequality. His political conclusions – that the labour movement must continue to show zeal in its transformative task – followed from these economic assumptions. However, this was not the predominant orthodoxy in the mid-1950s, even on the Left, for the continuation of the post-war boom was generally taken for granted.

In these circumstancess, Strachey became increasingly influenced by the prevailing intellectual mood. Instead of stressing the tension between the forces of political democracy and economic oligarchy, he simply implied that democracy had won the battle and that capitalism was now stable and controlled. He found a particular intellectual justification for this perspective in J. K. Galbraith's *The Affluent Society* published in 1958.

Strachey had been friendly with Galbraith for some years, having travelled to India with him in 1956, and having been in correspondence with him over economic issues since 1953. According to Galbraith, Strachey had even helped him with *The Affluent Society* by discussing the argument with him when he had reached an impasse.[19] Its theoretical content, therefore, came as no surprise, but he welcomed it with enthusiasm, predicting that it would become as influential as Keynes's *General Theory*. Galbraith assumed that the long-term future of capitalism as a stable and expanding system was assured, but pointed to the contradiction between 'private affluence and public squalor'. This helped to provide a rationale for Strachey to view Labour's task as the maintenance of a reasonable balance between the private and public sectors, while ensuring sufficient working-class purchasing power to maintain economic growth.[20]

Since concern about unemployment and instability had been so fundamental in Strachey's socialism, his belief that the fundamental problems of capitalism had been resolved was bound to have a major effect on his whole political perspectve. When writing *Contemporary Capitalism*, further steps towards socialism had been seen as necessary, but Strachey had been adamant that these must be achieved through political democracy. But, if further benefits for the working class could be secured within capitalism, the transformative element of political democracy became less important and the maintenance of the institutions themselves could be elevated as the goal.

The assumption that economic problems had been resolved not only increased the relative importance of the political domain but also transformed Strachey's approach to international issues. This was apparent not just in his attitude to war, where economic explanations were simply jettisoned but, still more remarkably, in his attitude to the nation-state itself. Thus, whereas in 1956 he had still regarded the maintenance of economic sovereignty as an imperative necessity, by 1961 he had become a committed supporter of British entry into the EEC. He welcomed this as a step towards the erosion of national sovereignty, which he now held to be anachronistic. He appears to have adopted this position without paying much regard to the economic issues involved because of his underlying assumption that economic growth would continue.

This elevation of the political dimension was also evident in his analysis of other systems. In India, for example, while naturally realising that there was an immense task of economic development to be carried out, he constantly praised the political system as the hope for democracy in the Third World. If this was a case of being over-impressed by the constitutional system, his attitude to the Soviet Union was, of course, the reverse. Here, Strachey minimised the economic development that had taken place since the Revolution – maintaining that the pace of industrialisation would have been similar under a non-Communist regime – and concentrated his whole attack on the lack of democracy.

This downgrading of economic issues was clearly crucial in the reconstitution of the intellectual framework in Strachey's political outlook. But this does not *explain* the change in position. Indeed, the fact that the shift was as much emotional as intellectual is apparent even if we do not, for the moment, look beyond economics. For Strachey never attempted to reconcile the economic theory of *Contemporary Capitalism* with the later assumption that the economic problems of capitalism had been resolved: he simply allowed these largely incompatible positions to coexist. This suggests that he *wanted* to adopt the new perspective because it now fitted in more easily with his general outlook. To understand this, it is necessary to consider other factors in his personality and political life.

In the last chapter we saw that, when writing *Contemporary Capitalism*, Strachey was preoccupied with reconciling his past and present positions. Its completion was cathartic in the sense that he never again needed to demonstrate the superiority of reformism over revolutionary Marxism: he could now simply assume that social democracy was valid and get on with his political life on Labour's front-bench. Yet this did not mean that he could escape his past. This was evident, above all, in his attitudes to democracy and Communism.

Strachey's fervent commitment to his restricted view of democracy was not really because of the 'lessons' of twentieth-century history. It was possible to be just as opposed to Fascism and Stalinism as Strachey himself, and yet to believe in a fuller and more radical version of participatory democracy. Of far greater importance was Strachey's *own* history: his own former passionate belief in two extra-parliamentary movements – the New Party and the Communist Party – followed by disillusionment and bitterness. It was this, coupled with the long-term elitist strain in his thought which accounted for his excessive attachment to political institutions and constitutions in the last years of his life. In other words, his narrow concept of democracy, which was evident not only in theory but also in his hostility to a new mass movement like CND, was largely explicable in terms of his alienation from his own past. This is still more manifest if his attitude to Communism is considered.

It is impossible to exaggerate the extent to which Strachey's general views in his last years were conditioned by his past and present attitudes to Communism. To a limited extent this resulted from his own experience of a contemporary event, for he was in Poland in October 1956 and witnessed the active revolt by workers against the regime. He came away more convinced than ever that the power of the state in Eastern Europe was based on repression alone and that democracy was of transcendent importance. The Hungarian uprising the next month, and the clear evidence that workers were being massacred in the interests of the Soviet State, reinforced these convictions. But his attitude to the present was inextricably bound up with his attempt to come to terms with his past: each new instance of Soviet repression was not merely a contemporary event, but 'Banquo's ghost'.

The trauma of the break with Communism was discussed extensively in Chapter 4. From 1942 until 1951 it had normally been repressed in activity, although the use of his Communist past in right-wing press attacks caused him considerable stress. After this, as shown in Chapter 6, he relived the 1930s by re-examining Marxist theory in *Contemporary Capitalism*.

The extent to which the whole Communist experience was still affecting him was poignantly expressed in a piece which Strachey wrote about Gollancz in 1954:

> like many others, he suffered intellectual and spiritual shipwreck, was drowned in the raging waters of our epoch, duly died, and was reborn with a new message for his fellow-men ...
>
> It is true that the bankruptcy of the Communist ideal in the West was not the sole cause ... of the subjective crises of the mid-twentieth century ... But for socialists ... what did the psychic damage were the horrors *in their own camp*. For they forced the rupture in those basic identifications which had been made ...
>
> Just as after a major war one sees *'les mutilés de guerre'* dragging themselves through the streets of a stricken country, so now the mutilated of the catastrophe of the Communist ideal in the West can be seen making their way across the face of Europe and the Americas. Such psychic mutilations are not indeed irreparable. There is a plastic surgery of the spirit by means of which men put themselves together again. But, of course, in so doing they become different.[21]

Because he was 'an unrepentant defender of human reason',[22] he tried to convince himself that both his past support for Communism and his current attitudes were 'rational'. In the 1930s, he maintained, it had been reasonable to accept the 'nightmarish features' in the Soviet Union as the only alternative to Fascism.[23]

But there had, in fact, been alternatives and he now claimed, as noted above, that the fundamental Communist mistake lay in its certainty.

In fact, he misinterpreted the basis of both his past and present attitudes. Had he really believed that there were 'nightmarish features' in Stalin's Soviet Union in the 1930s, it would mean that he had acted as a detached and cynical propagandist, who was prepared to paint a repressive dictatorship in glorious colours because it was the only alternative to Fascism. In fact, he had made some of his most excessive claims about the Soviet Union *before* Nazism had come to power in Germany and *before* Fascism had been seen as a universal tendency within capitalism. The Strachey of the 1930s had certainly believed Marxism–Leninism to be a rational, theoretical explanation of the world, but his attachement to Soviet-style Communism had also been deeply emotional.

The same kind of inadequacy was apparent in his belief that his current anti-Communism was rational. Had he been more dispassionate, he would not have seen its dogmatic certainty as the most fundamental cause of Stalinist terror. But he was far from dispassionate for, in reality, he was denouncing his own former 'certainty'. He, therefore, projected his anger at himself onto the former object of his passions. This meant that, even when he was prepared to accept that the Soviet Union was no longer 'a torture chamber', that it had a high growth rate, devoted a really adequate percentage of its gross national product to higher education and acted externally more or less in the same way as other countries, he could not forgive it. For Communist governments:

> must expect to be judged more strictly than the ordinary run of more or less purposeless, mediocre governments which have governed human societies at most times and in most places. It is the

> fate of the Communists to have produced the great disillusionment of the 20th Century. The fact that they have committed follies and crimes does not distinguish them from the rest of us. What makes it hard for our generation to forgive them is that they were once the hope of the world. Shakespeare put it 'lilies that fester smell far worse than weeds'.[24]

In terms of his own life, this attitude is understandable. But it also means that, in his last years, his professed arguments did not adequately explain his real attitudes. When he attacked absolutist anti-Communists for abandoning reason, it did not mean that his position was rationally based: because his religion was 'rationality' he desperately needed to 'rationalise' his convictions In fact, both his restricted view of Western democracy and his hope for change in the Soviet Union stemmed, in the final analysis, from his emotional rejection of Communism. The fact that this appeared a 'moderate' position and that his 'anti-Communism' was always expressed in the most restrained terms did not lessen the passions of the underlying convictions.

Through 'plastic surgery of the spirit' Strachey sought an escape fom his past by recasting himself as a conventional social democratic politician. In so doing, he shifted to the Right of the party and adopted the appropriate theoretical perspective for this position. It is not really surprising that he did so since he was not temperamentally suited for the relative isolation of the centre of the Labour Party – the position he had occupied between 1951 and 1955. For Strachey always sought some kind of security either in a doctrine (Marxism) or in a leader (Mosley). He had perhaps been happiest when the two had been combined during his Communist phase (an official doctrine, enforced through the Stalinist version of democratic centralism). For years after this he had sought certainty in 'a system which would embrace every aspect of knowledge'.[25] By now, he claimed that he had rejected the idea that any such theory was possible. If so, the security of allies and authorities became still more necessary and these could not be found in an ambivalent centrism.

If this further shift of position was not surprising (at least in retrospect), it was also almost inevitable that this time he would move to the Right. The impact that Communism had made upon him and the lasting trauma of the break made him recoil from the Left and seek a more conventional role. And he now transferred his faith in leaders onto Gaitskell and even George Brown. In doing this, he not only cut himself off from the beliefs and the people who had influenced him since the 1930s but he also reverted to a position more closely in line with his family background. He frequently referred to his father with affecion and respect and, in his last years, Strachey was to place a great deal of emphasis on the value of continuity in both personal and political terms.

Yet it is not clear that Strachey had settled into his new role so easily as this implies. In the first place, as a theoretician with a Marxist background, he was still an incongruous figure on the Right of the Labour Party and in the British liberal establishment. However attenuated his Marxism had become, it still acted as a barrier to complete acceptance by other Labour Party revisionists or by academics. It was, perhaps, partly for this reason that he turned to organisations like Radio Free Europe which welcomed his diluted Marxism as an extremely effective form of intellectual anti-Communism.

Secondly, despite the apparent tranquillity of his last years on Labour's Right, his activism and relentless search for a fully satisfying 'answer' to pressing problems were only just below the surface. In his attempt to refute unilateralism, for example, he convinced himself that the solution was world government, and attempted to persuade both the political elite and rank-and-file Labour members that it was imperative to work towards this ideal. This passion would probably have burnt itself out quite soon as he came to see that the obstacles were immense. In any case, it is probable that the Test Ban Treaty and the decline of CND activity would have ended his preoccupation with nuclear weapons. But it would, no doubt, have been replaced with a new search for truth and certainty and, in all probability, new authorities to confirm his views. And it is probably significant that just before he died (from a second heart attack, following an operation on his back), he began to read some theological works for the first time in his life.

By then, he was an author with an international reputation, and a well-known politician ready to assume a position in the cabinet of the next Labour government. He had, thus, achieved a great deal in his life. But it is unlikely that Strachey had found the certainty that he sought – or that he ever could have done.

8 Conclusion: Strachey today

When evaluating the historical contribution of individuals, it is normally relatively easy to decide whether to discuss their achievements in the realm of theory or action. In Britain, in particular, it is rare to consider someone who achieved prominence as a politician while constantly writing and providing theoretical appraisals of the political and economic world. When, as with Strachey, the individual's perspective changed several times over a forty-year period of active involvement in the labour movement, the difficulties are still greater. Should an evaluation look at these years as a theoretician of Communism or of revisionism? Should he be considered as a member of the ILP, the Labour Party Left, the Labour Party Right, the Communist Party or the New Party?

There is no doubt that Strachey's reputation has suffered as a result of such difficulties. He has been regarded as a maverick politician and as a derivative theorist. But even sympathetic critics have found him a problematic figure to assess. Was he primarily an activist or a theoretician; an extremist or a revisionist? Was he, above all, a writer who 'raised clarity of exposition to the point almost of genius'?[1] Or was he still more signficant – 'the one great socialist theoretician British Labour has yet produced'?[2]

In dealing with John Strachey, it often seems that there was not one man but several. In fact, however, there was a close relationship between the theorist and the political activist, and there was an underlying consistency in his fundamental preoccupations. The first point was put well by the French socialist, Jules Moch:

> Politicians can effectively be divided into four principal categories: those who think and act, those who think without acting, those who act without thinking, and those who neither think nor act ... John Strachey belongs, without any doubt, to the category of acting thinkers.[3]

Strachey was no detached intellectual: he never wanted simply to interpret the world but always also to change it. His wish for action fuelled his desire to understand and explain. Even if he was less significant as a politician than he was as a thinker, the relationship between the two aspects of his career was symbiotic. The writing could never have been so powerful and influential had it not been the work of a deeply committed political activist.

But if this political engagement increased the appeal of the writing, it may have prevented Strachey from developing into a still more signficant theoretician. He valued theory extremely highly, but he always regarded it as a servant to action, and also adopted new theoretical perspectives as his political position shifted. In the 1930s, for example, he developed some interesting and important insights into the relationship between psychology, language and political beliefs, but he did not sustain this concern once he moved away from revolutionary Marxism. Again, his later attempt to provide a synthesis between Marxism and Keynes was extremly significant but, once he thought the issue had been resolved in practice in a reformed capitalism, he took his research no further and turned to new fields, such as deterrence theory. However, if Strachey's active political involvement detracted from his ability to pursue sustained theoretical research on a particular theme, it made him still more significant as an individual: he was one of the very few prominent Labour politicians who have ever seriously tried to apply theoretical developments, across a wide range of social science, to political life.

Of course, he made serious mistakes and errors of judgement

in his career. He was often carried away by his emotional need for intellectual certainty and his tendency to defer to leaders. But, if there was only one Strachey, who tried to combine theory and action, it is also true that at a fundamental level he was far more consistent than his volatile political career implies.

He himself was aware that it was possible to have deep-rooted preoccupations and yet to act in ways which appeared inconsistent or contradictory. In the Preface to *The Coming Struggle for Power* he wrote:

> he who supposes that an Englishman of the present day can find his way either to intellectual certainty or political consistency, without doubts, hesitations and errors, shows little appreciation of the gravity or complexity of the present situation.[4]

Inconsistency could arise because the contradictions 'were in the objective situation itself as it ... developed historically'.[5]

His enduring preoccupations were encapsulated in his first book, *Revolution by Reason*. There, he argued that socialism was the ultimate solution to socio-economic problems, but that it was both possible and vital to implement an *immediate* programme of reforms to overcome the most pressing social ill: mass unemployment. Unless this was done, repression or chaos would ensue. Behind these convictions was the deep-seated assumption that liberal democracy contained virtues as well as vices. If full employment and the elimination of poverty could be achieved within capitalism, the peaceful, constitutional route to socialism would be vindicated. These were his permanent concerns, but his view of how change could be achieved shifted very considerably over time.

In the mid-1920s he saw the Labour Party as the agency for reform but rejected the notion of Fabian gradualism. The problems were so urgent that it was necessary to introduce a radical programme which could take immediate effect. Later in the decade he became intellectually converted to a form of Marxism, but still believed that it was possible to achieve some progress through the experience of a Labour government. However, the failure of the 1929 administration, amidst the most severe economic crisis of the twentieth century, led him to reject the Labour Party and seek support for an emergency programme in the New Party as the sole means of salvation. The evidence that this was leading to Fascism then forced him to reconsider his whole position. If, as he now thought, capitalism was doomed to ever greater crises, with poverty and unemployment for the masses, and there was no political agency which could bring about reforms, the sole alternative was Communism. The hope was that somehow the ensuing revolution would both end the miseries of capitalism *and* maintain 'civilisation'. Communism was, therefore, a last resort which he accepted only when absolutely convinced that all other routes to progress were barred. As soon as he came to believe that there was an alternative and that Communism was not, after all, the saviour, he headed back towards his pre-Communist beliefs, reinforced by Keynesian economics and his revulsion from 'totalitarianism'. This led to three closely inter-connected phases: the view (held between 1940 and 1945 and encapsulated in *A Programme for Progress*), that it was possible to reform capitalism with purposive government intervention; the belief (held during his years as a minister) that the post-war Labour government was implementing such a programme; and the theorisation (particularly in *Contemporary Capitalism*) of the specific circumstances and conditions in which capitalism might be controlled for the benefit of the wage-earning majority. Only in his last years did he become more complacent, believing that the goals that he had held since the 1920s had finally been realised: that unemployment and poverty had largely been conquered, and that it was possible to envisage a situation, short of socialism, in which working-class living standards could

Conclusion: Strachey today

rise constantly.

Strachey's preoccupations were thus consistent. Moreover, it is possible to understand why his political perspective could vary in accordance with historical circumstances and the development of economic theory. Naturally, his personality influenced his reading of the evidence, and the conclusions were never so clear as he believed. A less emotional person would not, for example, have followed Mosley in 1931, or have over-reacted against his experience of extra-parliamentary politics by adopting such a narrow view of democracy at the end of his life. Nevertheless, there was always some relationship between British politico-economic experience and Strachey's judgements of the needs of the time. This is not to suggest that his concept of socialism was ever fully rounded, for it was always restricted in crucial respects. In particular, it was predominantly masculine and elitist, and allowed little scope for mass participation, decentralisation or workers' control. However, in this sense too he reflected, in his own person, stages in the development of the British labour movement.

After his death, the manifestation of deep structural problems in the British economy, followed by the establishment of the radical-right Thatcher government in 1979 changed the para meters of British political life in a fundamental sense. The end of full employment, the introduction of privatisation, the increased economic inequality, the attack on the public sector and the decline of the labour movement have combined to undo the post-war settlement that had seemed to be so firmly based. On the bizarre assumptions that he had neither died in 1963 nor aged thereafter, what would Strachey have made of all this?

The first point to note is that he would have been less surprised than the overwhelming majority of political commentators. *Contemporary Capitalism* was characterised by his awareness of the underlying tensions in the system and the possibility that the post-war gains could be reversed if there was renewed economic instablility or a resurgence of right-wing Conservatism. He believed that this was unlikely but, even when he became increasingly confident about the stability of the system in his last years, he retained his historical perspective. In 1959, for example, he wrote:

> it is not in the least a question of the revolutionary tradition being wrong and the anti-revolutionary or reformist tradition being right or vice versa; it entirely depends on the objective development of the existing situation. If that development is . . . downwards towards crisis and catastrophe, then the reformist attitude is inapplicable; if contemporary development is, on balance, upwards towards a rising standard of life, continuous and effective remodelling of the system by democratic means with the avoidance of crisis and war, then, of course, the revolutionary tradition is inapplicable.

At the time he was quite convinced that: '. . . anyone who doubts that it is the revolutionary tradition that is inapplicable ought to have his head examined'. However, he stressed that:

> it is always extremely difficult to think oneself out of the mental climate of the particular period which one is in. I am now old enough to have seen the whole character of that mental climate change with the swiftly changing social environment more than once in the course of my lifetime. It is not very wise to assume as an axiom that it could never change again.[6]

This is not to suggest that the reappearance of mass unemployment and radical-right politics would have driven Strachey back towards a revolutionary perspective. He was so alienated from Communism that it is difficult to envisage circumstances in which he would again become so desperate about the possibility of peaceful change as to adopt the kind of stance which he had held in the 1930s. But, if he would have been able to understand 'Thatcherism' far more adequately than those without his historical and theoretical sophistication, how would he have *reacted* to it?

It is, of course, possible that he would simply have accepted it as an expression of the will of the electorate. Following the logic of his last years, he might have applied his restricted concept of democracy to Thatcherism so as to draw the following conclusions: regrettably, the people had rejected socialism and the labour movement must respect this choice and tailor its policies to the new climate of opinion.

But it is highly unlikely that he would have responded in this way to the new dominant ideology. First, his whole political life had been a struggle against unemployment and poverty. He saw the unemployed as the modern analogue of 'peasants with no hole in which to lay their heads' and full employment as '*by far*' the most important element in the programme of the post-war Labour government.[7] It is almost inconceivable that he would simply have recommended acquiescence in the dismantling of the post-war settlement. Secondly, his personality would not have led him to adopt an attitude of resignation in the face of the powerful forces that needed to be confronted. He was always convinced that, with a combination of determination and theoretical understanding, it was possible to act effectively in favour of the working classes. Thirdly, he was adamant in his rejection of the kind of *laissez-faire* economics with which the Conservative Right legitimised its assault on welfare capitalism. He believed that, as soon as economists had departed from the legacy of Ricardo and Marx and had introduced algebraic models of equilibrium analysis and concepts like marginal utility, they had headed down a blind alley:

> if we ask the blunt question, what was the value of the economists after they abandoned the search for value, we shall be bound to answer: something, but not very much.[8]

The idea of Strachey adopting the 'new realism' before market forces therefore contradicts his most fundamental preoccupations, and both emotional and theoretical sides of his personality. He would, I believe, have used all his energies to find a way of countering the new dominant perspective.

One element in this would have been at the level of ideology and, even in his last years, Strachey had much to say against materialism, the profit motive, individual self-interest, the neglect of the public sector and a narrowly functional view of education. A few years earlier he gave the important and relevant advice that the Labour Party must never lose sight of socialism as a goal and that arguments about efficiency degrade 'the cause of Socialism to the calculations of the cost accountant'.[9] It is also probable that, as in the 1930s, he would have tried to understand the mass psychology of radical-right rhetoric and to have framed a response in the kind of language which could have appealed to ordinary people.

Above all, he would surely have continued his lifelong work of trying to understand what was happening in the economy, and how it could be controlled and redirected for the benefit of the working classes. This was not because he regarded economics as more important than political, sociological, ideological or moral factors, but because economic health was a prerequisite for everything else. In particular, while he was, by the mid 1950s, convinced that issues of social morality were supreme, this very supremacy meant that he found it impossible to deal with them abstractly:

> For what has made men's efforts at social improvement so partially successful at best, and at worst so tragically abortive, has been insufficient comprehension of the ways and means by which their objectives may be reached . . .
>
> It is true that . . . economic and political questons . . . are not finally separable from those issues which turn upon a consideration of the

deepest springs of human action ... But ... I cannot even approach those supreme moral issues except by means of the study of the labyrinth of contemporary social reality. I can only attempt to catch a glimpse of what ought to be by means of achieving some degree of insight into what is.[10]

In the last part of the twentieth century, Strachey would have continued to believe that moral exhortation and ideological propaganda alone would be inadequate. Ultimately, the Left could triumph only if it also understood economic forces and the way in which they could be controlled politically. Even then, it must expect vehement opposition from capitalist interests.

How exactly he would have seen a way forward is unclear. It is unlikely that it would any longer have been primarily Keynesian or based on national economic sovereignty. For Strachey was always aware of historical change and in an era of international economic and financial power and British involvement in the EEC, demand management at nation-state level would no longer suffice. But Strachey's approach would be one of total determination to find a new synthesis between Marxist and non-Marxist political economy so as to define a new programme which could be implemented in practice.

Of course, all this is speculative and unprovable. It may appear excesssive to argue that a man whose judgement was often poor and whose political life was characterised by contradictions could have played a major role in clarifying the problems of the labour movement in the late twentieth century. Perhaps this is so. But few struggled as long and as hard as John Strachey to understand and control the political and economic forces at work in capitalism. And probably no-one was as successful at explaining theory to the Left and showing how it could be applied in practice. It is, therefore, not fanciful to suggest that this approach could have been beneficial for socialists grappling with the contemporary problems of the late twentieth century. As one of his obituary writers put it:

> John's intellectual integrity combined with a natural gentleness to prevent him from being a successful politician. He could neither accept nor produce the over-simplifications of party conflict. Cripps, Bevin, Nye Bevan and Gaitskell were all greater political figures, but nobody at all equalled the intellectual contribution which John Strachey made to democratic socialism both here and throughout the world.[11]

Notes

Preface
1 Michael Foot, *Tribune*, 19 July 1963.
2 Richard Crossman, the *Manchester Guardian*, 19 July 1963.

Chapter 1
1 Amabel Williams Ellis, *All Stracheys are Cousins*, Weidenfeld & Nicolson (1983), p. 8.
2 Amy Strachey, *St. Loe Strachey – His Life and his Paper*, Gollancz (1930), p. 363.
3 'The education of a Communist', *Left Review*, December 1934.
4 Quoted in Hugh Thomas, *John Strachey*, Eyre Methuen (1973), p. 24, (hereafter Thomas).
5 Fenner Brockway, *Inside the Left*, Allen & Unwin (1942), p. 146.
6 *Socialist Review* March 1926.
7 *Inside the Left*, pp. 145-6.
8 *Socialist Review* October 1924.
9 The *Spectator,* 20 September 1924.
10 *Revolution by Reason*, Leonard Parsons (1925).
11 *Ibid.*, p. vii and 253.
12 *Ibid.*, p. 105.
13 *Ibid.*, p. 128.
14 Dalton to Strachey, 3 January 1926, Strachey Papers (hereafter SP).
15 *The New Leader* (Conference Supplement), 9 April 1926.
16 F. M. Leventhal, *The Last Dissenter: H. N. Brailsford and his World*, Oxford University Press (1985), p. 191.
17 *Labour Magazine*, February 1926.
18 *Socialist Review*, February 1926.
19 *Revolution by Reason*, p. 256.
20. *Socialist Review*, July 1928.
21 *Ibid.*, August 1928.
22 *Ibid.*, November and December 1927.
23 *Ibid.*, August 1928.
24 *Ibid.*, July 1927.

25 *Ibid.*, April and May 1929.
26 *Ibid.*, October 1928.
27 *Ibid.*, June 1929.
28 *Aston Labour News*, 25 May 1929.

Chapter 2

1 *New Leader*, 4 October 1929, cited in S. McIntyre 'John Strachey 1901-31: The Development of an English Marxist', unpublished MA thesis, Monash University, Australia (1971), p. 108 (hereafter McIntyre).
2 Robert Skidelsky's *Politicians and the Slump*, Penguin (1970) and *Oswald Mosley*, Macmillan (1975), are extremely thorough on the Mosley Memorandum and have provided a great deal of information for this chapter.
3 Skidelsky, *Mosley*, p. 209.
4 *Weekend Review*, 22 March 1930.
5 Skidelsky, *Mosley*, p. 213.
6 *Daily Herald*, 30 May 1930, quoted in McIntyre, p. 123.
7 *Socialist Review*, July 1928.
8 *Hansard*, vol. 231, cols 957-61, 5 November 1929.
9 Skidelsky, *Mosley*, p. 235.
10 *Hansard*, vol. 244, cols 169-74, 29 October 1930.
11 Skidelsky, *Mosley,* pp. 238-9.
12 *Ibid.*, pp. 236-7.
13 *Hansard*, vol. 246, cols 1352-4, 17 December 1930.
14 *Town Crier* (Birmingham), 19 December 1930, quoted in Thomas, p. 92.
15 Michael Foot, *Aneurin Bevan, Vol. 1, 1897-1945, Four Square*, (1966), p. 110.
16 Skidelsky, *Mosley*, p. 242.
17 *Manchester Guardian*, 25 February 1931, quoted in McIntyre, p. 147.
18 *A National Policy*, Macmillan (1931), pp. 6-7.
19 *Ibid.*, p. 47.
20 *Weekend Review*, 20 June 1931.
21 'Parliamentary reform: The New Party's proposals', *Political Quarterly*, 2 (3), July-September 1931.
22 *The Menace of Fascism*, Gollancz (1933), p. 161 (hereafter *Menace*).
23 *Weekend Review*, 20 June 1931.
24 Thomas, p. 105.
25 Foot, *Bevan, Vol. 1*, p. 114.
26 Bevan to Strachey, 29 July 1931, SP (also quoted in Thomas, pp. 107-8.

27 'Birmingham Labour and the New Party', *Labour Magazine*, April 1931.
28 *Menace*, p. 162.
29 *Ibid.*

Chapter 3

1 'The education of a Communist' *Left Review*, December 1934.
2 *The Coming Struggle for Power*, Gollancz (1932), p. 66 (hereafter *Struggle*).
3 'The education of a Communist'.
4 Strachey to Dutt, 24 December 1931, SP.
5 Strachey to Dutt, 16 November 1932, SP.
6 Strachey to Dutt, 24 April 1933, SP.
7 For a recent full discussion of Gollancz and the Left Book Club, see Ruth Dudley Edwards, *Victor Gollancz*, Gollancz (1987).
8 *What Are We To Do?*, Gollancz (1938), p. 258.
9 Boothby to Strachey, 7 November 1932, quoted in Thomas, p. 133.
10 John Lewis, *The Left Book Club*, Gollancz (1970), p. 37.
11 *Struggle*, p. 297.
12 *Ibid.*, p. 302
13 *Ibid.*, p. 321
14 *Ibid.*, pp. 337-8.
15 *Ibid.*, pp. 165-6.
16 *Ibid.*, p. 185.
17 *Ibid.*, p. 198.
18 *Ibid.*, p. 215-16.
19 *Ibid.*, pp. 396-6.
20 *Ibid.*, p. 356.
21 *Ibid.*, pp. 358-9.
22 J. K. Galbraith, 'John Strachey', *Encounter*, September 1963.
23 'John Strachey and the Left Book Club' (1956), in Richard Crossman, *The Charm of Politics*, Hamish Hamilton (1958), p. 140.
24 *Democracy versus Dictatorship: British Labour's Call to the people*, National Joint Council (1933).
25 Strachey to Dutt, 23 June 1933, SP.
26 Strachey to Gollancz, 23 April 1933, SP.
27 *Menace*, p. 130.
28 *Ibid.*, p. 244.
29 *Ibid.*, p. 246.
30 *Ibid.*, p. 247.

31 *Ibid.*, p. 272.
32 *The Nature of Capitalist Crisis*, Gollancz (1935), pp. 145-6.
33 Hugh Delargy, *Sunday Citizen*, 21 July 1963.
34 'On Gollancz' (1954), in *The Strangled Cry*, Bodley Head (1962), p. 220.
35 Richard Crossman, 'John Strachey and the Left Book Club', pp. 140-1.
36 Strachey to J. K. Murray, 17 August 1934, SP.
37 Strachey to Gollancz, 12 October 1934, SP.
38 'The education of a Communist'.
39 Preface to R. Osborne's *Freud and Marx*, Gollancz (1937), pp. 13-14.
40 *Ibid.*, p. 15.
41 Strachey to Sir Evelyn Wrench, 6 October 1933, SP.
42 *The Theory and Practice of Socialism*, Gollancz (1936), p. 408.
43 Preface, *Freud and Marx*, pp. 17-18.
44 *What Are We To Do?*, pp. 228-9.
45 *Ibid.*, p. 385.
46 Max Lerner, in *Book Union Bulletin* (New York), November 1936.
47 D. Mirsky, *The Intelligentsia of Great Britain*, Gollancz (1935) p. 233.
48 'The education of a Communist'.

Chapter 4

1 Strachey to Dutt, 6 May 1940, SP (also quoted in Thomas, p. 196).
2 J. K. Galbraith, *Encounter*, September 1963,
3 Thomas, p. 197.
4 Strachey to Sir Evelyn Wrench, 6 October 1933, SP.
5 Strachey to Boothby, 2 October 1938, SP (also quoted in Thomas, p. 178).
6 Strachey to Boothby, 25 August 1939 SP (also quoted in Thomas, p. 184).
7 Quoted in Noreen Branson, *History of the Communist Party of Great Britain, 1927-41*, Lawrence & Wishart (1985), p. 286.
8 *New Statesman*, 27 April 1940 (also quoted in Thomas, p. 192).
9 *Post-D*, Gollancz (1941), p. 135.
10 Strachey to Ivor Montagu, 16 August 1940, SP.
11 *The Frontiers*, Gollancz (1952) p. 144. (Government censors would not allow the novel to be published during the war.)
12 *The Nature of Capitalist Crisis*, pp. 295-5 (hereafter *Capitalist Crisis*).
13 Strachey to Sir Richard Acland, 29 September 1937, SP.
14 Strachey to Donald Carroll, April 1938, SP. (Thomas quotes extensively from this fascinating letter, pp. 170-2.)
15 Strachey to Dutt, 19 May 1938, SP.

16 *Ibid.*
17 *New Fabian Research Bureau Quarterly*, Summer 1938, quoted in Ben Pimlott, *Labour and the Left in the 1930s*, Cambridge University Press (1977), p. 40.
18 'John Strachey and the Left Book Club', p. 142.
19 Douglas Jay to Strachey, 20 August 1938, SP.
20 Evan Durbin to Strachey, 1 March 1940, SP.
21 *A Programme for Progress*, Gollancz (1940), pp. 153–4 (hereafter *Programme*).
22 *Capitalist Crisis*, p. 97.
23 *Ibid.*
24 *Programme*, p. 128.
25 *Ibid.*, p. 334.
26 *Ibid.*, p. 335.
27 *Ibid.*, p. 334.
28 *Ibid.*, p. 38.
29 *Ibid.*, p. 151.
30 *Ibid.*, p. 7.
31 *Ibid.*, p. 159.
32 *Ibid.*, p. 295.
33 *Ibid.*, p. 164.
34 Strachey to Donald Klopfer, 13 March 1940, SP.
35 Emile Burns to Strachey, 14 November 1939, SP.
36 *Daily Worker*, 2 March 1940.
37 Strachey to Dutt, 6 May 1940, SP.
38 Strachey to a CP comrade, 25 January 1940, SP.
39 Strachey to Evan Durbin, 23 February 1940, SP.
40 'Proposal for a new association', February 1942, SP.
41 Letter to Celia (undated), 1942, SP.
42 *Ibid.*
43 *Ibid.*
44 'Proposal for a new association'.
45 *Ibid.*
46 Letter to Celia. (The role of the Labour Party was implicit in this letter.)

Chapter 5

1 The *Observer*, 22 July 1963.
2 Kenneth O. Morgan, *Labour in Power, 1945–51*, Oxford University Press (1985), p. 494. (This excellent book is the most authoritative source on the Attlee governments and has provided much of the information for

this chapter.)
3 CAB 134/176, Minutes of Emergencies Committee, 4 and 6 July 1949. (All government papers cited in this chapter are to be found in the Public Records Office, Kew.)
4 Strachey to government Chief Whip, 20 July 1949, SP.
5 'Notes and comments on Toynbee's Study of History', September 1949, SP.
6 *Ibid.*
7 *Ibid.*
8 *Ibid.*
9 Strachey to Attlee, 5 July 1946, SP.
10 *The Diary of Hugh Gaitskell* (ed. Philip Williams), Jonathan Cape (1983), p. 25, entry of 12 August 1947.
11 CAB 128 CM(46), Confidential Annex to Conclusions, 21 July 1946.
12 Memorandum for EPC, 10 September 1948 in PREM 8 1412, Part 1.
13 *Change and Fortune*, Hutchinson (1980), p. 179 (and personal interview).
14 Morgan, p. 363.
15 Memorandum for EPC, 16 May 1949, in PREM 8 1412, Part 1.
16 These judgements are tentative since there is no thorough and objective study of the scheme. The most useful account is Alan Wood, *The Groundnut Affair*, Bodley Head (1950). However, this is not impartial since Wood had been chief public relations officer for the project until he resigned in September 1949.
17 CAB 128, 13 January 1947.
18 CAB 128, 19 January 1948.
19 Wood, *The Groundnut Affair*, p. 100.
20 *Ibid.*, p. 200.
21 *Ibid.*, p. 215.
22 CAB 128, 14 November 1949.
23 CAB 128, 7 December 1950.
24 Strachey to the Director-General of Food and Agriculture at the United Nations, 19 May 1950, SP.
25 CAB 128, 14 November, 1949.
26 *The End of Empire*, Gollancz (1959), p. 184.
27 'Democratic socialism', *Tribune*, 23 February 1950.
28 'The Economic Prospect', lecture to Fabian Conference, 14-15 October 1950. (This lecture formed the basis for the talk delivered to the Fabian conference in October 1951, which was subsequently published as 'Tasks and achievements of British Labour', in R. Crossman (ed.), *New Fabian*

Essays, Turnstile Press [1952].)
29 CAB 128/18 1 August 1950, cited in Morgan, p. 424.
30 Strachey to Attlee 'Anglo-American Relations', 2 January 1951, SP.
31 Strachey to Field Marshal Sir William J. Slim, CIGS, 20 July 1950, SP.
32 Dalton's Diary, 9 February 1951, quoted in Morgan, p. 434.
33 Strachey to Attlee, 2 January, 1951, SP.
34 SP (also mentioned in Thomas, pp. 264-5).
35 Speech at Enfield, 23 July 1950, SP.
36 Strachey to Attlee, 23 April 1951, SP.
37 Speech in Dundee, 29 April 1951, SP.
38 Strachey to Shinwell (undated), July 1951, SP.
39 Speech in Laurencekirk, 28 July 1951, SP.
40 Attlee's private secretary to Strachey, 25 July 1951, SP.
41 Speech in Laurencekirk.
42 Attlee to Strachey, 3 December 1951.

Chapter 6

1 Richard Crossman *Crossman, Backbench Diaries* (ed. Janet Morgan), Hamish Hamilton and Jonathan Cape (1981), Diary entry of 11 May 1954, pp. 327-8.
2 'The Passionate moderate', *Daily Herald*, 4 April 1952.
3 'Marxism revisited' (4 articles), *New Statesman*, 2, 9, 16 and 23 May 1953.
4 'The light of common day', unpublished chapter, SP.
5 Strachey to Donald Klopfer, 28 December 1955, SP.
6 This is my own brief summary of the changes that he identified early in the book which appear the most crucial for his subsequent analysis. His own summary is in *Contemporary Capitalism*, Gollancz (1956), pp. 26-40.
7 *Ibid.*, p. 31.
8 *Ibid.*, p. 41.
9 *Ibid.*, p. 40.
10 Marx, *Capital*, Vol.1, chapter 24 (quoted in *Contemporary Capitalism*, p. 101).
11 *Contemporary Capitalism*, p. 94.
12 *Ibid.*, p. 150.
13 *Ibid.*, p. 151.
14 *Ibid.*, p. 154-5.
15 *Ibid.*, p. 179.
16 *Ibid.*, p. 180.
17 *Ibid.*, p. 238.

18 *Ibid.*, p. 246n.
19 *Ibid.*, p. 260.
20 *Ibid.*, p. 262.
21 *Ibid.*, p. 269-72.
22 *Ibid.*, p. 272.
23 *Ibid.*, p. 283-4.
24 *Ibid.*, p. 286.
25 *Ibid.*, p. 287.
26 *Ibid.*, p. 290.
27 *Ibid.*, p. 290n.
28 *Ibid.*, p. 292.
29 See p. 000. His first extensive discussion of the crucial importance of maintaining economic sovereignty was in *Federalism or Socialism?*, Gollancz (1940) and he had adhered to this view ever since.
30 'The powder and the jam' *New Statesman*, 6 February 1954.
31 *Ibid.*
32 Strachey to Gaitskell, 11 February 1954, SP (also quoted in Thomas, pp. 273-4).
33 'The British experiment (cont.): a social ejection mechanism', unpublished chapter, SP.
34 *Ibid.*
35 *Ibid.*
36 Strachey to P. J. Sills, 25 September 1956, SP.
37 'A social ejection mechanism'.
38 Strachey to Donald Klopfer, 28 December 1955. (Unfortunately Gaitskell's letter is not in Strachey's papers and Gaitskell's papers were not available.)
39 Saxe Commins to Strachey, 30 August 1956, SP. (In the American edition all references to 'last stage capitalism' were changed to 'latest stage of capitalism'.)
40 Letter to Strachey, 7 May 1956.
41 'Socialist literature in the 1950s', *Political Quarterly*, 31(3), July-September 1060.
42 See, for example, Stephen Haseler, *The Gaitskellites: Revisionism in the British Labour Party, 1951-–64*, Macmillan (1969).
43 6 October 1956.
44 Mohit Sen, in *New Age* (India), April 1957.
45 *New Statesman*, 6 February 1954.

Chapter 7

1. *The Challenge of Democracy*, Encounter Pamphlet no. 10 (1963).
2. 'Lenin in April', in George Urban (ed.), *Talking to Eastern Europe*, Eyre & Spottiswood (1964).
3. 'The blackwater: a study in depth', unpublished, SP.
4. 'A new kind of social democracy', written on 24 November 1959 for publication in *Asaki Journal* (Japan).
5. 'The unreaped harvest', *Sunday Times*, 23 January 1963.
6. Strachey to Gollancz, 28 December 1961, SP.
7. Strachey to Douglas Hyde, 7 March 1961, SP.
8. Raymond Fletcher, *Tribune*, 27 November 1959.
9. 'J. K. Galbraith: the book' (1958), in *The Strangled Cry*, Bodley Head (1962), p. 210.
10. *Challenge of Democracy*, p. 13.
11. 'A Politician's View of Democracy', paper at International Seminar, Rhodes, 6-13 October 1958 under the auspices of Congress for Cultural Freedom, SP.
12. *Challenge of Democracy*, p. 2.
13. *Contemporary Capitalism*, p. 163.
14. *Challenge of Democracy*, pp. 23-4.
15. 'Lenin in April', p. 25.
16. His most extensive discussion of these issues was in *On the Prevention of War*, Macmillan (1962).
17. Strachey to Herman Kahn, 8 March 1960, SP.
18. Richard Crossman, The *Guardian*, 28 September 1962 (review of *On the Prevention of War*).
19. J. K. Galbraith, *Encounter*, September 1963.
20. 'J. K. Galbraith 1 (1958) and 2 (1961)' in *The Strangled Cry*.
21. 'Victor Gollancz' (1954), in *The Strangled Cry*, pp. 219-20.
22. Strachey to K. M. Panikkar, 2 April 1963, SP.
23. *The Strangled Cry*, pp. 17 and 188.
24. *Challenge of Democracy*, p. 36.
25. Michael Foot, *Tribune*, 19 July 1963.

Chapter 8

1. Michael Foot, *Tribune*, 19 July 1963.
2. Flavius, *New Statesman*, 19 July 1963.
3. Preface to the French edition to *The End of Empire*.

4 Preface to the first edition of *The Coming Struggle for Power*.
5 'Laski', *The Strangled Cry*, pp. 196-7.
6 Undated draft article (1959) on Professor Homan for *New Statesman*.
7 'Notes on Toynbee's Study of History', (1949), SP.
8 *Contemporary Capitalism*, p. 77.
9 'The object of further socialisation', undated, 1952/3, SP.
10 *Contemporary Capitalism*, pp. 17-18.
11 R. Paget, *The Times*, 17 July 1963.

Further reading

Unfortunately, most of Strachey's books are now out of print and are not easily available. This is very regrettable since they are a major source not only for his own thought but also for that of the British Left as a whole. His papers, which were indispensable for this book, are in the possession of his family.

The only previous biography is that of Hugh Thomas, *John Strachey*, Eyre Methuen (1973). This is thorough and informative, and was very useful for my own research. However, it appears neither sympathetic to, nor even very interested in, his ideas. The only other recent discussion of Strachey as a theorist is Stuart McIntyre, 'John Strachey, 1930-31: The Development of an English Marxist', MA thesis, Monash University, Australia (1971). This is an important study but is, unfortunately, unpublished.

Strachey's major writings are listed below along with a small selection of secondary works which either discuss Strachey explicitly or provide significant contextual material. Strachey wrote an enormous number of articles over a forty-year period, as well as editing *Socialist Review* and the *Miner* from 1926 to 1929. In the 1920s he contributed regularly to the *Spectator* and the *New Leader*; in the 1930s to *Labour Monthly*, the *Daily Worker* and the *Left News* in Britain, and *New Masses* in the USA; and in the post-war period he often wrote for the *New Statesman*, the *Daily Herald* and a variety of other journals and newspapers including, ultimately, *Encounter*. His articles are not included here, but references are given in the notes to each chapter, and also in Hugh Thomas's biography. Those who are interested in his early journalism should refer to Stuart Macintyre's thesis, which includes a list of his major political articles up to 1931.

Books by Strachey

The following is a list of Strachey's books and longer pamphlets, in chronological order, with the date of the original British publication. Most of his books were also published in the USA, sometimes with the inclusion of material of specific American interest. Two short books were published solely in the USA:
Literature and Dialectical Materialism Covici, Friede (1934).
Hope in America, Modern Age Books (1938)

Revolution by Reason, Leonard Parsons (1925)
(With A. Bevan and G. Strauss), *What We Saw in Russia*, Hogarth Press (pamphlet 1931)

Further reading

(with A. Bevan, W. J. Brown and A. Young), *A National Policy: An Account of the Emergency Programme Advanced by Sir Oswald Mosley, M.P.* (pamphlet), Macmillan (1931).
The Coming Struggle for Power, Gollancz (1932).
The Menace of Fascism, Gollancz (1933).
The Nature of Capitalist Crisis, Gollancz (1935).
The Theory and Practice of Socialism, Gollancz (1936).
What Are We To Do?, Gollancz (1938)
Why You Should be a Socialist, Gollancz (pamphlet 1938).
A Programme for Progress, Gollancz (1940).
Banks for the People, Gollancz (pamphlet 1940).
Federalism or Socialism, Gollancz (1940).
A Faith to Fight For, Gollancz (1941).
Victor Gollancz (ed.), *The Betrayal of the Left*, Gollancz (1941).
Post-D: Some Experiences of an Air Raid Warden, Gollancz (1941).
The Frontiers, Gollancz (a novel, 1952, written in 1941).
The Just Society: A Re-Affirmation of Faith in Socialism, Labour Party (pamphlet 1951).
Contemporary Capitalism, Gollancz (1956).
Scrap ALL the H-Bombs, Labour Party (pamphlet 1958).
The End of Empire, Gollancz (1959).
The Pursuit of Peace, Fabian Tract 329 (pamphlet 1960).
The Great Awakening, Encounter Pamphlet No. 5 (pamphlet 1962).
The Strangled Cry, Bodley Head (1962).
On the Prevention of War, Macmillan, (1962).
The Challenge of Democracy, Encounter Pamphlet no. 10 (pamphlet 1963).

Secondary sources

R. Barker, *Political Ideas in Modern Britain*, Methuen (1978).
Noreen Branson, *History of the Communist Party of Great Britain, 1926-41)*. Lawrence and Wishart (1985).
Fenner Brockway, *Inside the Left*, Allen & Unwin (1942).
J. Campbell, *Nye Bevan and the Mirage of British Socialism*, Weidenfeld & Nicolson (1987).
Bernard Crick, 'Socialist literature in the 1950s', *Political Quarterly*, 31 (3), July-September 1960.
C. A. R. Crosland, *The Future of Socialism*, Jonathan Cape (1956).
Richard Crossman, *New Fabian Essays*, Turnstile Press (1952). (This includes a chapter by Strachey, 'Tasks and achievements of British labour'.)
——, *The Charm of Politics*, Hamish Hamilton (1958).
——, *Backbench Diaries*, (ed. Janet Morgan), Hamish Hamilton & Jonathan Cape (1981).
Robert Dowse, *Left in the Centre: The Independent Labour Party, 1893–1940*, Longmans (1966).
Elizabeth Durbin, *New Jerusalems*, Routledge (1985).

Further reading

Ruth Dudley Edwards, *Victor Gollancz*, Gollancz (1987).
Michael Foot, *Aneurin Bevan, Vol. 1, 1897-1945*, Four Square (1966).
——, *Aneurin Bevan, Vol. 2, 1945-60*, Paladin (1975).
——, *Loyalists and Loners*, Collins (1986).
Geoffrey Foote, *The Labour Party's Political Thought – A History*, Croom Helm (1985).
Stephen Haseler, *The Gaitskellites: Revisionism in the British Labour Party, 1951–64*, Macmillen (1969).
David Howell, *British Social Democracy*, Croom Helm (1976).
Douglas Jay, *Change and Fortune*, Hutchinson (1980).
F. M. Leventhal, *The Last Dissenter: H. N. Brailsford and his World*, Oxford University Press (1985).
John Lewis, *The Left Book Club*, Gollancz (1970).
Stuart Macintyre, *A Proletarian Science: Marxism in Britain, 1917-33)*, Lawrence & Wishart (1986).
Kenneth O. Morgan, *Labour in Power, 1945-51)*, Oxford University Press (1985).
Ben Pimlott, *Labour and the Left in the 1930s*, Cambridge University Press (1977).
——, *Hugh Dalton*, Jonathan Cape (1985).
Patricia Pugh, *Educate, Agitate and Organise: 100 years of Fabian Socialism*, Methuen (1984).
Robert Skidelsky, *Politicians and the Slump: The Labour Government Of 1929-31*, Penguin (1970).
——, *Oswald Mosley*, Macmillan (1975).
Philip Williams, *Hugh Gaitskell*, Jonathan Cape (1979).
—— (ed.), *The Diary of Hugh Gaitskell*, Jonathan Cape (1983).
Neil Wood, *Communism and British Intellectuals*, Gollancz (1959).
Anthony Wright, *British Socialism: Socialist Thought from the 1880s to 1960s*, Longman (1983).
—— (ed.), *Socialisms*, Oxford University Press (1986).

Index

Abyssinia, 61
Affluent society, The (1958) (Galbraith), 170-1
Africa, 111-18 *Passim*
Allen, Clifford, 16
Allen, W. E. D., 38
arms control, 168; expenditure, 39, 88, 121-7, 131, 132, 141
Asia, 151
Attlee, Clement, 103, 106-9 *passim*, 115, 116, 120, 121, 123-6 *passim*, 128, 129, 132
Austria, 66

Baldwin, Oliver, 38
Bank of England, 12, 23
banking system, 12-14 *passim*, 19, 87, 93, 94, 102
Bernstein, Eduard, 153
Betrayal of the Left, The (1941) (Strachey), 83
Bevan, Aneurin, 31-4 *passim*, 37, 38, 43-5 *passim*, 47, 105, 106, 121, 122, 125-8, 131-3 *passim*, 188
Bevin, Ernest, 105, 188
'Birmingham proposals', 8-15, 17, 27
Birmingham Trade Union Emergency Committee, 18
Bodley Head, The, 158
Boothby, Robert, 3, 7, 24, 30, 32, 55, 78, 79

Brailsford, H. N., 15
Brandt Report, 161
Brockway, Fenner, 4, 5
Brown, George, 177
Brown, W. J., 31, 34, 38
Burns, Emile, 96

Cambridge University Social Democratic society, 157
capital, export of, 93, 147, 149, 150
capitalism, 7, 8, 14, 19-20, 23, 28, 50, 52, 53, 57-8, 60-5 *passim*, 69, 71, 73-4, 78-9, 84-97, 99, 102, 104, 135-54, 159-60, 162-4, 170-1, 180, 182
children's allowances, 93
China, 121, 123-5 *passim*
Churchill, Winston, 42
Clause 4, 156-7
CND, 158, 166-7, 173, 178
coal, 13, 17-18; and steel community, 120
Coming Struggle for Power, The (1932) (Strachey), 54, 56-62, 66, 67, 74-5, 181
Comintern, 79, 98
Commonwealth, 32, 35, 38, 155, 161-2
Communism, 21-2, 24, 48-55, 68-78, 81, 82, 84-7, 95-9 *passim*, 102, 105-7 *passim*, 120, 121, 123, 134,

203

Index

142-4, 156, 161, 165-6, 173-7, 182, 184
Communist International, 21-2, 52, 53, 98
Communist Party, 16, 21-2, 24, 31, 47-9, 51-3 *passim*, 56, 62, 72, 73, 77, 79-87 *passim*, 95-9, 120, 173, 179
Congress for Cultural Freedom, 158
Conservative Party, 26, 27, 31, 114-16 *passim*, 119, 132, 133, 142, 184, 185
Contemporary Capitalism (1956) (Strachey), 134-48, 150-4, 155, 161-5 *passim*, 169-72 *passim*, 174, 182, 183
controls, economic 23, 35, 38, 93, 119, 146-50, 153, 182 *see also* rationing
Cook, A. J., 19, 35, 42
'Cook–Maxton Manifesto', 20
Creech-Jones, Arthur, 111, 112, 115, 117, 118
Cripps, Sir Stafford, 100, 105, 110, 114, 188
Crick, Bernard, 151
Crosland, Anthony, 151-3, 163
Crossman, Richard, 62, 67, 87-8, 168

Daily Worker 49, 80, 96
Dalton, Hugh, 14, 15, 108, 111, 112.
decolonisation, 155, 161-2
defence policy, 121-7, 131, 132, 155, 166-8 *see also* deterrence: nuclear weapons; rearmament
Democracy versus Dictatorship (1933), 62-3, 65

Denmark, 80
deterrence, nuclear, 157, 167, 180.
devaluation, 106
development, economic, 160, 161, 172
disarmament, nuclear, 156, 157, 168 *see also* CND
Dobb, Maurice, 95, 153
Durbin, Elizabeth, 88
Durbin, Evan, 88
Dutt, R. Palme, 21, 52, 77, 80, 86, 97

Economic Policy Committee, 108, 110
economic theory, 7-16, 30-1, 38-9, 84-102, 135-54, 162-3, 170, 172, 182, 186-7
Economist, The, 116
EEC, 169, 171, 187
employment, 10, 87, 93, 94, 96, 104, 107, 136-8 *passim*, 146, 181, 183, 185 *see also* unemployment
Encounter, 156, 158
End of Empire, The (1959) (Strachey), 135, 155, 159-62
Engels, Frederick, 22, 70, 100
Europe, 56, 61, 104, 120-1, 131, 138, 151, 157, *see also* EEC; Eastern, 161, 173
Evening Standard, 120
Everyman, 78

Fabianism, 10-11, 14, 181
family background, 1-3
Fascism, 27, 39-41 *passim*, 46, 47, 52-3, 55, 56, 58, 61-4 *passim*, 66, 71-3, 82-3, 85-7 *passim*, 94, 95,

204

Index

100, 135, 173-5 *passim*, 182 see also *Menace of, The;* British Union of Fascists, 27, 52, 65; World Committee against War and, 52, 65
Finland, 80
food supplies, 109 *see also* rationing
Foot, Michael, 120
Fouquet, Yvette, 3-4, 5
France, 43, 66, 80, 93, 150
Franco, General Francisco, 61
Freeman, John, 122
Freud, Sigmund, 70
Freud and Marx (1937) (Osborne), 70, 72
Frontiers, The (1952) (Strachey), 83
Fuchs, Klaus, 120
Future of Socialism, The (1956) (Crosland), 151-3

Gaitskell, Hugh, 106, 122, 124-6 *passim*, 131, 132, 148, 150, 154, 155, 157, 168, 169, 177, 188
Galbraith, J. K., 61-2, 170-1
General Theory (Keynes), 87-8, 171
George V, King, 26
George, David Lloyd, 42.
Germany, 51, 52, 61, 64, 65, 79, 98, 109, 121, 123, 124, 131, 135, 142, 166, 175; pact with Soviet Union (1939), 79, 82.
Gold Standard, 9, 10, 12
Gollancz, Victor, 53-4, 56-7, 68, 100, 101, 158, 174
groundnuts, 111-18, 130

Hayek, Friedrich, 90, 91.

Hitler, Adolf, 51, 52, 67, 80, 81
Hobson, John, 11, 15
Hong Kong, 123
housing, 6
Hungary, 62, 173

imperialism, 11, 32, 33, 35, 39, 58, 80, 135, 159-62
Independent Labour Party (ILP), 4, 5, 8, 11, 14-17, 20-22 *passim*, 32, 33, 35-6, 179
India, 109, 155, 160, 162, 170, 172
inflation, 12, 91, 93
interest rates, 88, 92
investment, 38, 58, 88, 92, 140 *see also* public works
Italy, 61, 62, 65, 79

Japan, 61, 151
Jay, Douglas, 88, 110
Jenkins, Roy, 157
Jews, 63, 105
Joad, Professor, 40, 42.
Johnson, J., 44-5

Keynes, J. M./Keynesianism, 7, 10, 12, 16, 86-9 *passim*, 92, 97, 99, 140-1, 180, 182, 187
Korea, 121 *see also* war, Korean.

Labour Government, 14, 23-4, 150, 182, (1924), 6, 8, 10, 16; (1929), 26, 36-7, 47, 49-50, 87, 94; (1945), 88, 103-30, 147-9, 161, 185
Labour Party, 2, 5, 6, 8-10 *passim*, 15, 16, 18, 20-3 *passim*, 26, 31, 32, 39,

Index

43, 44, 47, 53, 62-4 *passim*, 67, 78, 96, 101-2, 105, 130-3, 151-3, 156, 157, 161, 167-9, 176-7, 179, 181-2, 186; ideology in 105, 131-3; Parliamentary, 16, 18-19, 31, 34-7 *passim*, 108, 132
Laski, Harold, 54, 101
Latin America, 151
Left Book Club, 54-7, 67, 70
Left News, 54
Lenin, Vladimir Ilyich/Leninism, 11, 22, 100, 101, 156, 160
Liberal Party, 6, 26, 31, 96
Living Wage, 14-15

McArthur, General, 121, 124, 125, 127
MacDonald, Ramsey, 6, 15, 16, 20, 26, 37, 50, 129
Macmillan, Harold, 32
Manchester Guardian, 30
Manchuria, 61
Marx, Karl, 7, 22, 70, 89, 107, 137-9 *passim*, 185
Marxism, 10, 19-22, 24, 28, 45, 48, 51, 55, 68-9, 70, 72, 73, 83, 84, 97-100, 102, 133, 135, 137-41, 143, 149, 152, 153, 159, 160, 174-7 *passim*, 180, 182, 187
'Marxism Revisited' (1953) (Strachey), 133
Maxton, James, 16, 20, 36
Menace of Fascism, The (1933) (Strachey), 63-6, 71
Mills, C. Wright, 151
Miner, The, 19, 21
Mirsky, Dimitri, 75

Moch, Jules, 179-80
Mond–Turner talks, 18, 20
monetary policy, 12, 14, 15, 30, 90-4, 102
Morel, E. D., 4
Morgan, Kenneth O., 104
Morris, Sir Wiliam, 37
Morrison, Herbert, 65, 109, 132
Mosley, Sir Oswald, 7-14, 16, 27-47 *passim*, 129, 169, 176, 183; Manifesto, 34-6; Memorandum, 30-3
Munich crisis, 78
Murphy, Esther (wife), 24, 47, 51
Mussolini, Benito, 3
Myrdal, Gunnar, 160

National Health Service, 104, 122, 126
National Government, 65
National Policy, A (1931), 38, 43
nationalisation, 11, 12, 14, 15, 31, 104, 105, 128, 131, 148
NATO, 104
Nature of Capitalist Crisis, The (1935) (Strachey), 66, 84, 85, 90
Nazism, 47, 52, 61, 63, 66, 72, 83, 94, 99, 101, 166, 175
Nehru, Jawaharlal, 155
New Deal, 89, 91, 99
New Jerusalems (1985) (Durbin), 88
New Leader, 4
New Party, 27, 38-47 *passim*, 75, 173, 179, 182
New Statesman, 77, 80, 133, 147, 153
non-proliferation, 167-8
Norway, 80
nuclear weapons, 121, 125, 166-7, 178 *see also* non-proliferation

Index

On the Prevention of War (1962) (Strachey), 155-6, 158
Osborne, R. 70, 73
Overseas Food Corporation, 113-16
ownership, public, 12, 32, 128, 147, 153, 157, 163 *see also* Clause 4; nationalisation

pact, German–Soviet, 79, 82
Palestine, 105
patriotism, 78-82
pensions, old age, 30, 93
planning, economic, 34-5, 38, 58
Plummer, Leslie, 113-17 *passim*
Poland, 173
political theory, 18-19, 22-4, 30-1, 36, 39-40, 42, 45-6, 49-50, 52-62, 68-9, 71-4, 83, 97-104 *passim*, 119, 140-5, 147, 151-6 *passim*, 158-62, 163-6, 171-3, 183-5
Pollitt, Harry, 80
Ponsonby, Arthur, 4
Ponsonby, Elizabeth, 4
popular fronts, 52-6 *passim*, 78, 84, 86, 93, 95-8 *passim*
Prices and Production (1931) (Hayek), 90
Problems and Perils of Socialism (1908) (St Loe Strachey), 2
Programme for Progress, A (1940) (Strachey), 87-97, 104, 139, 182
protectionism, 32, 38
psychology, 69-73 *passim*, 85, 180
public works, 35, 38, 88, 89, 92

Radio Free Europe, 158, 177
RAF, 82, 103, 107
rationing food, 108-11, 130

rearmament, 121-7 *passim*, 131; German, 121, 123, 124, 131
Reich, Wilhelm, 72
revolution, 9, 60-3, 102, 107, 134, 159, 182, 184
Revolution by Reason (1925) (Mosley), 8; (Strachey), 8, 14-17, 19, 94, 181
Ricardo, David, 137, 185
Rosa, John, 115
Roosevelt, President, F. D., 86, 91

Schuman, Robert, 120
Schuman, Plan, 147
science, 59
Senior, Nassau, 1, 7
Shawcross, Hartley, 120
Shinwell, Emmanuel, 109, 119, 124, 127
Simpson, Celia (wife), 47, 50, 51, 55, 74, 99, 101, 158
Smith, Ben, 111
Snowden, Philip, 16, 29, 36
Socialism and the Living Wage (1927) (Dutt), 21
Socialist Review, 16-17, 20
Soviet Union, 19, 21, 28, 32-3, 39, 43, 53, 61, 62, 66, 68, 79-82 *passim*, 98, 99, 105, 121-4 *passim*, 161, 165-6, 172-6 *passim*; pact with Germany (1939), 79, 82
Spain, 61, 62, 66
Spectator, 1, 3, 51, 78
Stalin, Josef, 32, 68
Stalinism, 173, 175, 176
state intervention, 136, 182 *see also Programme for Progress*; public works
steel, 13, 105; coal and steel community, 120

Index

Strachey, Amabel (sister), 2
Strachey, Amy (mother), 3, 5, 25
Strachey, James (cousin), 1
Strachey, Lytton (cousin), 1
Strachey, St Loe (father), 1-3 *passim*, 7
Strangled Cry, The (1960) (Strachey), 156, 158
Strauss, George, 33
strikes, 17-19, 106, 164; General, 18-19
Study of History, A (Tonybee), 103
Sweden, 99

Tanganyika, 111-18 *passim*
taxation, 13, 88, 92, 163
Test Ban Treaty, 168, 178
textiles, 13
Thatcherism, 146, 183, 185-6
Theory and Practice of Socialism, The (1936) (Strachey), 56, 57, 68, 71
Third World, 131, 160-1, 172
Thomas, Hugh, 77
Thomas, J. H., 29-31 *passim*
Times, The, 116
Toynbee, Arnold, 103
Tract on Monetary Reform (Keynes), 12
trade, 9, 32, 35, 38, 39, 43 *see also* protectionism
Trade Disputes Act (1927), 18
trade unions, 15, 18, 63, 105, 131, 136, 139
Tribune, 120, 161
TUC, 17, 18, 20

'under-consumption', 11, 12, 14, 15, 92
unemployment, 6, 7, 9, 10, 11, 15, 26-30 *passim*, 33-4, 37, 43, 58, 61, 87, 92-4 *passim*, 102, 171, 181, 182, 184, 185; relief, 10, 13, 26, 42
unilateralism, 157, 166-8. 177
Unilever 111
Union for Democratic Control, 4
United Africa Company, 111, 113
united front, 52, 53, 62, 64, 67 *see also* popular fronts
United Nations, 121
USA, 43, 48-50 *passim*, 56, 61, 91, 121, 123-5 *passim*, 127, 131, 135, 138, 151, 157-8, 161

wages, 10, 13, 15, 64, 91, 92, 137-9, 149
Wakefield, John, 111, 112, 115
Wall Street Crash, 29
war, 58, 60, 61, 85, 122-3, 167; Cold, 135, 166; Korean, 121-8 *passim*; Manchurian, 61; Spanish Civil, 66; World, first, 9; second, 79-83 *passim*, 85, 96, 97, 166
Webb Maurice, 116, 117
What We Saw In Russia (1931) (Strachey, Bevan & Strauss), 33
Wheatley, John, 6
Why You Should be a Socialist (1938) (Strachey), 56, 57
Wilson, Harold, 122
World Committee against War and Fascism, 52, 65

Young, Allan, 38, 40, 41, 43, 46, 100, 101
youth movement, 41-2